projects for small gardens

projects for small gardens

56 projects with step-by-step instructions

Richard Bird

George Carter

photography by
Jonathan Buckley
Marianne Majerus
Stephen Robson

RYLAND
PETERS
& SMALL

LONDON NEW YORK

For this edition:
Senior designer Sally Powell
Senior editor Clare Double
Picture researcher Emily Westlake
Production Paul Harding, Deborah Wehner
Art director Anne-Marie Bulat
Editorial director Julia Charles
Consultant David Grist

Illustration David Atkinson, Richard Bonson, Martine Collings,
Tracy Fennell, Valerie Hill, Stephen Hird, Sarah Kensington,
Sally Launder, Amanda Patton, Elizabeth Pepperell, Lizzie
Sanders, Helen Smythe, Ann Winterbotham

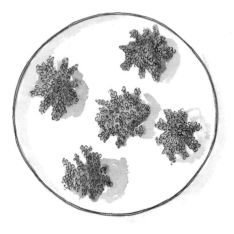

First published in the United States in 2002
This edition published in 2006 by Ryland Peters & Small
519 Broadway, 5th Floor, New York, NY 10012
www.rylandpeters.com
10 9 8 7 6 5 4 3 2

Text © Richard Bird 1998, 2000, 2002, 2006
and George Carter 1997, 2002, 2006
Design, illustrations and photographs © Ryland
Peters & Small 1997, 1998, 2000, 2002, 2006

ISBN-10: 1-84597-124-8
ISBN-13: 978-1-84597-124-3

The original edition was cataloged as follows.
  Library of Congress Cataloging-in-Publication Data
Bird, Richard.
  Projects for small gardens / by Richard Bird and
George Carter.
    p. cm.
  ISBN 1-84172-266-9
  1. Garden ornaments and furniture.
  2. Garden structures. I. Carter, George, 1948– II. Title.
  SB473.5. B57 2002
  648.1'8--dc21   2001048853

Printed and bound in China

contents

introduction 6
containers to make 8
a wood and trellis camouflage box 10
a Versailles case 14
planted gate piers 18
a trough with trellis screen 22
an herbal window box 26
a chamomile seat 30
a raised scented window box 34
balcony herb boxes 38
galvanized buckets 42

decorated containers 46
a shell-faced trough 48
a lead-faced trough 52
a rustic window box 56
a circular pipe with flowering tree 60
a painted galvanized washtub 64
terra cotta with a patina 68
painted pots 72

brickwork & stone projects 76
a small brick-edged herb garden 78
a brickwork trough 82
brick raised beds 86
a raised flower bed 90
an herb-lined pathway 94
a retaining wall 98
a wall cascade 102

wood & metal garden structures 106
a trellis screen 108
a rustic trellis 112
a trellis-enclosed herb garden 116
vertical planting 120
a scented arbor 124
a wooden obelisk 128
miniature hurdles 132

a picket fence 136
wattle panels 140
a checkerboard parterre 144
herb staging 148
a primula theater 152
a wirework basket 156
a rose arch 160

decorative planting projects 164
a scented knot garden 166
corner planting 170
a sweet pea obelisk 174
a honeysuckle porch 178
a rose growing through a tree 182
a scented path 186
herb topiary 190

edible planting projects 194
baskets of tomatoes 196
chile peppers in pots 200
a patio container garden 204
fruit trees in pots 208
culinary herb half-barrels 212
an edible border 216
a salad bed 220
a strawberry bed 224
a taste of Asia 228
herbs in a mixed bed 232
a potager 236
a bean arbor 240

tools and techniques 244
care and maintenance 254
useful addresses 262
credits 265
index 266
acknowledgments 272

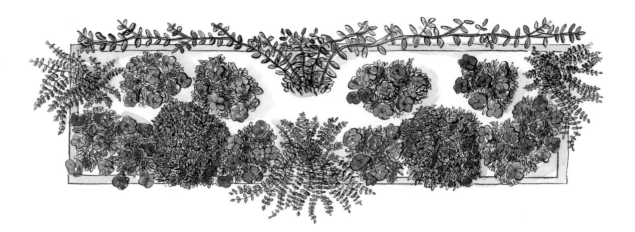

Designing or redesigning even the smallest garden can appear daunting when considered as a whole, but if it is approached as a series of projects the prospect at once seems more manageable. Of course, you need to devise an overall plan for a garden before attempting individual projects—but, once this has been done, then each area can be tackled in your own time.

Many of the projects in this book add a structural element that would suit any small garden, whether formal, informal, or natural in character. Most gardens can benefit from containers that provide year-round focal points, such as the Versailles Case shown on pages 14–17, especially when planted with an evergreen shrub. Taller structures such as arches and arbors also play an important role in small gardens by meeting the need for height when the space for trees is limited. The Vertical Planting project on pages 120–123 shows how to make the most of walls for growing plants when space for horizontal planting is restricted.

In addition to projects involving building or construction, there are plenty of ideas for exciting and unusual planting plans, both decorative and edible, in beds or containers, some of which are suitable for a roof garden, a balcony, or even a windowsill.

containers
to make

a wood and trellis camouflage box

This container is designed to mask plants in plastic pots for seasonally changing arrangements. There is no base—simply fit it over your potted plants. A useful disguise for pots, the box also allows you to mix plants with different soil and feeding requirements.

MATERIALS & EQUIPMENT

2 pieces exterior-grade plywood ³⁄₄ x 15 x 24 in (20 x 380 x 600 mm)

2 pieces exterior-grade plywood ³⁄₄ x 15 x 22½ in (20 x 380 x 560 mm)

4 pieces surfaced softwood 2 x 2 x 30 in [1 x 2] (50 x 50 x 750 mm)

44 ft (13.6 m) surfaced softwood for lattice ½ x 1 in (10 x 25 mm)

1 quart (1 liter) each exterior-grade wood preservative and exterior-grade latex paint

galvanized finishing nails 2 in (50 mm) and 1 in (25 mm)

waterproof carpenter's glue

no. 8 screws 2 in (50 mm)

16 standard-sized bricks

4 marguerites (*Argyranthemum frutescens*) in 10 in (250 mm) plastic pots

1 To assemble the sides of the box, place the ends of the shorter boards against the inside face of the longer ones; glue in place, then reinforce with 2 in (50 mm) finishing nails. Mark a line 2 in (50 mm) from the top all the way around the box; the lattice will be fixed below this line.

To apply the lattice to the outside of the box, follow steps 2, 3, 4, and 5 for each of the four sides.

2 Measure and cut a length of lattice to form a diagonal strut. Lay it against the side of the box with its center line on the center line of the diagonal. Mark and miter the ends to match the corners of the box. Repeat for the other diagonal but cut a piece from the middle of the strut to fit. Glue and nail with 1 in (25 mm) finishing nails.

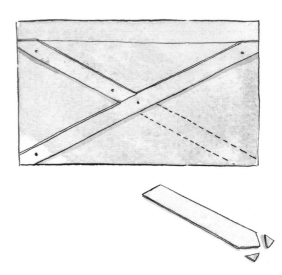

3 Use a pencil to mark the center points of each side at the edges. These marks will serve as guides for the accurate construction of the central lozenge shape.

4 Make the first of the four diamond struts by placing a section of lattice in a line from a top or bottom center mark to a side mark. Cut a piece from the middle of this so it fits around the piece already in place and miter the ends.

5 Repeat step 4 for the other diagonals and fit them together on the box, matching the mitered ends. Glue and nail into place.

6 Treat all surfaces, inside and outside, with wood preservative and allow it to dry.

7 To form the top molding, miter the ends of the four pieces of 1 x 2 so they fit together snugly around the top edge of the box.

8 Drill screw holes along the top edges, then screw the molding to the box from the inside so it lies flush with the top edges. Reinforce the mitered corners with finishing nails. Coat the molding with wood preservative.

9 Apply two coats of paint in the color of your choice to the inside and outside of the box.

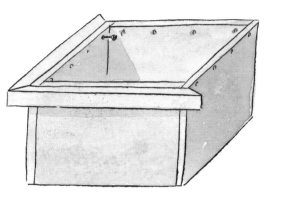

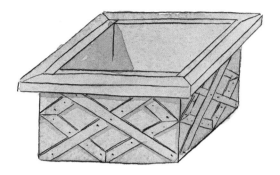

10 You may need to create a platform to make sure the tops of the pots rest just below the top of the molding. In this project two layers of four bricks have been placed under each of the pots so the pots sit ½ in (10 mm) below the top edge of the container; leave small gaps between the bricks to allow for drainage.

11 Place the plastic pots inside the container, one on each block of bricks. Marguerites have been chosen for this display because their mass of foliage and flowers works well with the proportions of the box.

alternative planting plans
4 *Fuchsia* x *speciosa* 'La Bianca,' 4 *Daphne odorata* 'Aureomarginata,' 4 common ivy (*Hedera helix* 'Erecta') around a common boxwood (*Buxus sempervirens*), 4 bear's breeches (*Acanthus mollis*), or 4 *Camellia japonica*.

a Versailles case

A Versailles case is a wooden box that was used at the Palace of Versailles, in France, in the 17th century for growing exotics such as oranges, lemons, and palms, which could then be easily moved into the orangery or the greenhouses during the winter. A Versailles case can be unscrewed when the plants need repotting, or used as a decorative exterior for housing plants in plastic boxes or pots.

MATERIALS & EQUIPMENT

rough-sawn lumber (see step 1, page 16)

4 finials, balls, or pyramids with ½ in (10 mm) diameter dowels

1 piece of exterior-grade plywood ½ x 13¼ x 13¼ in (10 x 375 x 375 mm)

no. 8 screws 2 in (50 mm) and 1½ in (40 mm)

waterproof carpenter's glue

1 quart (1 liter) exterior-grade wood preservative

wood stain or exterior-grade latex paint

pot shards

50 quarts (50 liters) potting soil (approximately)

New Zealand tea tree (*Leptospermum scoparium*)

1   Cut the following in rough-sawn lumber:
- 6 side boards ¾ x 5½ x 15 in [1 x 6]
  (25 x 150 x 380 mm)
- 6 side boards ¾ x 5½ x 16½ in [1 x 6]
  (25 x 150 x 430 mm)
- 4 side supports 2 x 2 x 19½ in [2 x 2]
  (50 x 50 x 525 mm)
- 4 base supports 1 x 1 x 12 in [2 x 2]
  (25 x 25 x 280 mm)

2   Drill pilot holes in each corner of the six shorter side boards about ¾ in (20 mm) from the edge. The holes should be made to fit the 2 in (50 mm) screws. Do the same with the six longer side boards.

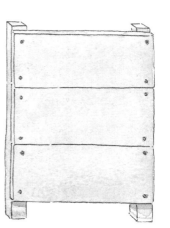

3   Using 2 in (50 mm) screws, attach the shorter boards to the side supports, flush to the edge, with a 2 in (50 mm) projection at the bottom and a 1 in (25 mm) projection at the top.

4   Using 2 in (50 mm) screws, attach the longer boards to the outside face of each of the side supports, creating a square-ended butt joint.

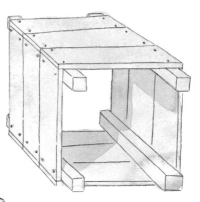

5   Prepare the base supports for 1½ in (40 mm) screws by drilling a hole about 1 in (25 mm) from each end. Place one support between each of the four side supports inside the box, positioning them at the base, flush with the bottom board. Screw into place.

6   To fit the base, cut a 1¾ in (45 mm) square from each corner of the piece of plywood. Using a power drill with a 1 in (25 mm) spade bit, make five drainage holes, positioning them as shown. Drop the base into the case from the top; it should rest on the base supports secured in step 5.

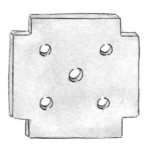

7 To attach the finials, drill in the top of each upright a ½ in (10 mm) diameter hole for the dowel, positioning it in the center. Use waterproof glue to secure the finial in the hole.

Alternatively, make your own finials, putting them in place as shown on a separate 2 in (50 mm) dowel. Suitable designs for this size of case include a 2 in (50 mm) diameter wooden ball and a 5 in (130 mm) high pyramid cut from a 2 x 2 in (50 x 50 mm) rod. Place the pyramid atop a slightly smaller block.

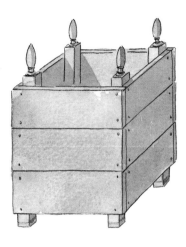

8 To protect the case, coat it in wood preservative inside and out. Then apply a wood stain or paint. Make sure the paint is thoroughly dry before planting up.

9 Line the base of the case with pot shards. Take the plant from its pot and tease out the roots. Center the tree in the case and add moistened potting soil until the tree and surrounding soil are about 1½ in (40 mm) from the top of the case.

A flowering tea tree has been used here, but Versailles cases are also suitable for large shrubs, topiary, and masses of summer annuals.

10 After the tree has flowered, trim the outer leaves to keep the ball shape.

planted gate piers

It is often useful to be able to raise plants up high so they can be appreciated
from a distance. Use the planters in pairs to resemble gateposts or as part of a screen
to mark a division in the garden. These wooden gate piers have been designed as
cachepots—the individual plants remain in their plastic pots and can
be changed seasonally.

MATERIALS & EQUIPMENT

1 piece exterior-grade plywood ½ x 48 x 96 in (10 x 1200 x 2400 mm)

2 pieces exterior-grade plywood ½ x 11½ x 11½ in (10 x 290 x 290 mm)

rough-sawn lumber (see steps 2, 3, 5, and 6, pages 20–21)

2½ quarts (2½ liters) each exterior-grade wood preservative and exterior-grade latex paint

waterproof carpenter's glue

galvanized finishing nails 2 in (50 mm)

galvanized nails 1½ in (40 mm)

no. 8 screws 1¼ in (30 mm) and 3 in (75 mm)

4 *Hydrangea macrophylla*

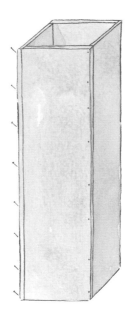

1 Cut the large piece of plywood into eight equal pieces, each measuring 12 x 48 in (300 x 1200 mm). Using butt joints, make two boxes by gluing the end of each board to the inside face of another; use finishing nails inserted at a slight angle.

2 For the base supports, use the 1½ x 1½ x 11½ in (40 x 40 x 290 mm) lumber. Position two battens on the inside of each box, opposite one another and 9 in (230 mm) from the top. Drill holes in the plywood for 1¼ in (30 mm) screws. Glue the battens in place and secure with screws.

3 To make the top moldings, cut four pieces of ¾ x 2½ x 17½ in (50 x 50 x 410 mm) lumber for each pier. Miter the corners (see page 247). Glue and nail moldings in place flush with the top edge and finish by reinforcing the mitered corners with finishing nails.

4 Treat the gate piers inside and out with wood preservative, making sure you coat the base thoroughly. When it has dried, apply two coats of paint to the outside and the inside down to the level of the base supports.

If the gate piers are to be placed on soil, follow step 5. To attach them to concrete or paving, skip to step 6.

5 Make eight supporting stakes from rough-sawn lumber, each measuring 1½ x 1½ x 18 in [2 x 2] (40 x 40 x 450 mm); sharpen one end on each to form a point. For each pier, hammer four stakes into the soil, spacing them to fit into the inside corners; the internal dimensions of the pier are 11½ in (290 mm) square. Leave at least 6–8 in (150–200 mm) of stake above the soil. Lower each pier over the stakes to sit on the ground and use a level to check that the pier is vertical. If the surface is uneven, bank it up with soil so the tops of both piers are level. Drill holes for 1¼ in (30 mm) screws in the bottom corners of the pier and screw the stakes to the plywood structure.

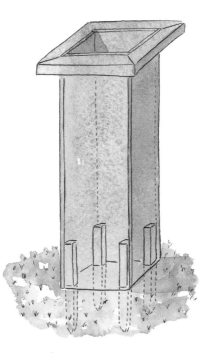

6 To fix the piers to concrete, first cut four battens from rough-sawn lumber, each measuring 1½ x 1½ x 11½ in [2 x 2] (40 x 40 x 290 mm). Using two for each pier, place them opposite one another with the outside edges 11½ in (290 mm) apart. Using masonry or concrete fasteners and the appropriate drill bit, fasten the battens to the surface. Place the piers over the battens. Check they are level. Drill holes for 3 in (75 mm) screws and screw the piers to the battens through the sides.

7 Make the two plant shelves from the remaining squares of plywood. Using a power drill with a 1 in (25 mm) spade bit, drill five drainage holes. Treat both squares with wood preservative before dropping them onto the supporting battens inside each pier.

8 The gate piers are now ready to be planted by placing the potted plants directly onto the plant shelves. Hydrangeas have been used for this project, but the height of the base and pier can be adjusted to suit plants of different sizes and shapes.

alternative planting plan
Other plants that would be suitable for this arrangement include a ball of boxwood (*Buxus sempervirens*) or marguerites (*Argyranthemum frutescens*). Keep all plants fed and watered according to their individual needs.

a trough with trellis screen

This versatile trellis-backed trough is essentially a portable container for
tall plants and climbers and can be moved around whenever you want
to change your garden layout. It acts as both a screen and a planter and
is ideal for use on a balcony or a rooftop garden where it may
be difficult to support posts.

MATERIALS & EQUIPMENT

rough-sawn lumber (see step 1, page 24)

no. 8 screws 1½ in (40 mm), 2½ in (65 mm), and 4 in (100 mm)

galvanized finishing nails 1 in (25 mm)

1 piece exterior-grade plywood ¾ x 13¾ x 33¾ in (20 x 345 x 845 mm)

45 ft (13.7 m) surfaced softwood ¾ x 1¼ in [1 x 2] (20 x 30 mm)

1 quart (1 liter) exterior-grade wood preservative and about 2½ quarts (2½ liters) stain

pot shards

50 quarts (50 liters) potting soil (approximately)

1 *Trachelospermum jasminoides*

2 creeping myrtle (*Vinca minor*)

3 sky-blue creeping myrtle (*Vinca minor* 'Azurea Flore Plena')

10 *Petunia* 'Dark Blue Dwarf'

1 Cut the following pieces in rough-sawn lumber:
- 4 pieces for sides ¾ x 5½ x 14 in [1 x 6]
  (20 x 150 x 350 mm)
- 4 pieces for front and back ¾ x 5½ x 36 in [1 x 6]
  (20 x 150 x 900 mm)
- 4 uprights 2 x 2 x 12 in [2 x 2] (50 x 50 x 300 mm)
- 2 battens 1 x 1 x 31½ in [2 x 2] (25 x 25 x 750 mm)
- 2 battens 1 x 1 x 11 in [2 x 2] (25 x 25 x 250 mm)
- 2 trellis supports 2 x 2 x 68 in [2 x 2]
  (50 x 50 x 1700 mm)

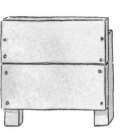

2 Drill holes for 2 in (50 mm) screws at both ends of the side boards. Use two boards for each side and screw them to the side supports, lining up the outer edges and staggering them so that two 2 in (50 mm) legs protrude from the bottom.

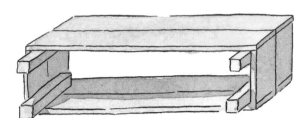

3 Assemble the box by screwing the front and back boards to the outside face of the sides; drill holes and use 2½ in (65 mm) screws to secure the joints.

4 Drill the battens for the 1½ in (40 mm) screws and place the battens between the uprights on the inside, flush with the base. Secure them in place with screws.

5 For the base, cut a 1¾ x 1¾ in (50 x 50 mm) square from each corner of the piece of plywood. Using a power drill with a 1 in (25 mm) spade bit, drill five drainage holes in the plywood. Slide the base into position atop the battens.

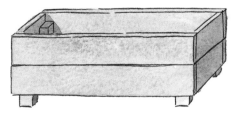

6 Treat the box and base with wood preservative. When it has dried, apply a couple of coats of stain.

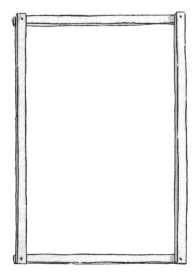

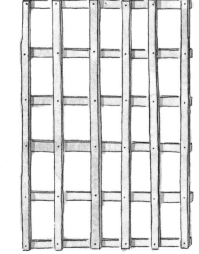

7 To make the trellis panel, use the 45 ft of 1 x 2 lumber to make six 54 in (1.35 m) and six 36 in (900 mm) pieces. Start by making a rectangular frame: nail two of the shorter sections behind the longer ones, flush with the ends.

8 Divide each side into five equal parts and mark the divisions with a pencil. Nail the vertical sections of trellis first, top and bottom, and then the horizontals behind these, nailing at all junctions. Treat the structure and the trellis supports with preservative.

9 Drill the trellis supports for 2½ in (65 mm) screws and place them against the back of the trellis, flush with the top and sides. Screw in place from the front. Stain the trellis and supports.

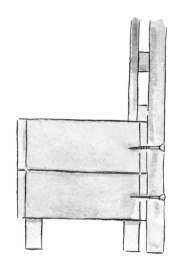

10 To join trough and trellis, drill holes in the trellis supports for 4 in (100 mm) screws; position the holes so that the screws will go through the trellis and the side supports inside the trough. Make sure all sides and bottom edges line up and screw the pieces together.

11 Line the trough with pot shards and enough moistened potting soil to ensure that the top of the plants are about 1 in (25 mm) from the top edge. Use a tall trained jasmine for this project; if your plants are small, use two.

12 Place the plant in the center at the back of the trough, tease out the individual stems, and arrange them on the front of the trellis as evenly as possible; tie them to the trellis with coated wire.

13 Place the creeping myrtle along the length of the trough and fill in the spaces with dark blue petunias. Water thoroughly, and follow up with a liquid fertilizer every two weeks or so.

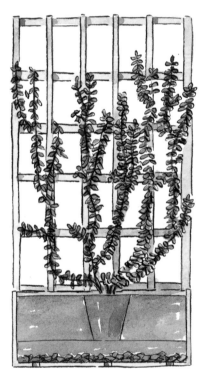

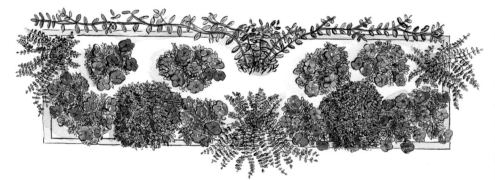

alternative planting plan
For a colder climate, plant the semi-evergreen wall shrub *Pyracantha coccinea*, underplanted with *Hedera helix*. For the trellis backing you could also use a more hedgelike plant such as a hawthorn or holly or even *Aucuba japonica*, which thrives even in very polluted environments.

an herbal window box

This window box will allow you to grow herbs for the kitchen even in a very confined space. The color scheme used here is based on golden sage, purple basil, and cream oregano. If you prefer to grow other herbs, you can devise your own scheme— for example, a symmetrical planting plan using a combination of shrubby and trailing herbs as well as a good contrast of colors creates a particularly decorative effect.

MATERIALS & EQUIPMENT

1 window box 11 x 11½ x 31 in (250 x 300 x 780 mm) (see page 246)

45 in (1.1 m) surfaced softwood for lattice ¼ x 1⅜ in (6 x 20 mm)

90 in (2.25 m) surfaced softwood for molding ¾ x 1½ in [1 x 2] (20 x 40 mm)

no. 8 screws 2 in (50 mm) and 1½ in (40 mm)

galvanized finishing nails ¾ in (20 mm)

waterproof carpenter's glue

1 quart (1 liter) each exterior-grade wood preservative and
wood stain (light green/gray color)

pot shards

50 quarts (50 liters) potting soil (approximately)

1 plastic pot

pot-grown herbs (see page 29)

1   The window box can be bought from a garden center or made at home. If you want to make the box yourself, see page 246 for the quantities and measurements of lumber.

2   To attach the fretwork, cut three 10¼ in (260 mm) vertical battens from the lattice. Glue and nail them to the front of the box so they sit ¾ in (20 mm) from the top of the box. Cut four 13¼ in (360 mm) horizontal battens to fit between the vertical battens.

3   To attach the cross fretwork, cut four 18 in (450 mm) battens from the lattice wood. Hold two of the battens in front of the box on the diagonal, as shown. Mark the pointed angles with a pencil so that the battens will fit within the vertical and horizontal battens. Cut, glue, and nail into place.

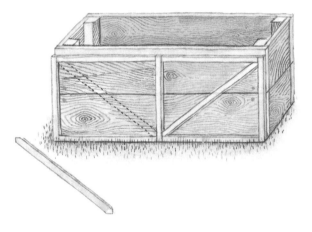

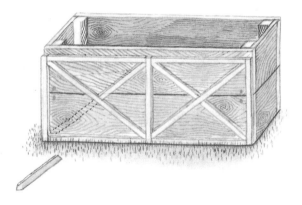

4   To create the crossed pattern, cut two more 18 in (450 mm) battens. Cut them in half, then cut them to fit, as in step 3. Glue, nail, and wipe off any excess glue.

5   To make the moldings, start by cutting four pieces of 1 x 2 (20 x 40 mm) lumber to the following lengths: one 33½ in (840 mm) for the front, one 31 in (780 mm) for the back, and two 12½ in (310 mm) for the sides. Leave the back and one end of the side moldings straight; miter all others (see page 247). Attach from the inside with 2 in (50 mm) screws. Apply wood preservative and let dry before applying the stain.

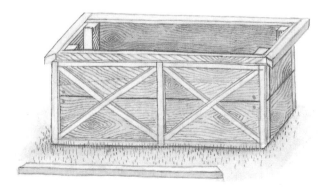

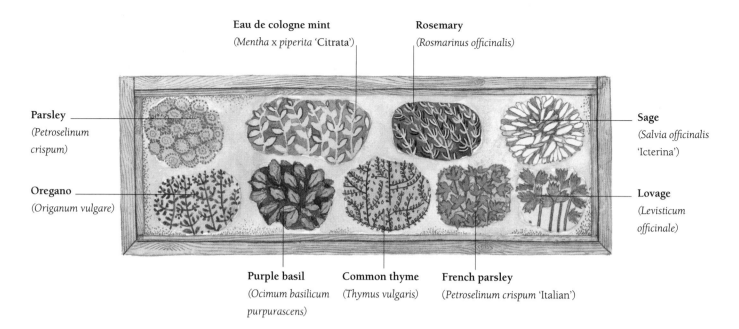

Eau de cologne mint
(*Mentha* x *piperita* 'Citrata')

Rosemary
(*Rosmarinus officinalis*)

Parsley
(*Petroselinum*
crispum)

Sage
(*Salvia officinalis*
'Icterina')

Oregano
(*Origanum vulgare*)

Lovage
(*Levisticum*
officinale)

Purple basil
(*Ocimum basilicum*
purpurascens)

Common thyme
(*Thymus vulgaris*)

French parsley
(*Petroselinum crispum* 'Italian')

6 When the stain is dry, line the bottom of the window box with pot shards. Take the plants from their pots and tease out the roots. Because mint is aggressive, plant it in the plastic pot, which can be plunged into the soil. Arrange the plants as shown in the illustration and add moistened potting soil until the plants and the surrounding soil are about 1½ in (40 mm) from the top of the window box.

a chamomile seat

Turf seats—consisting of a raised bed made from willow hurdles, bricks, or lumber planks—have their origins in medieval gardens. Planted with aromatic herbs, such as chamomile, or mown grass, they provide a pleasantly fragrant and comfortable seating area. Such seats were often placed in a niche or in a wooden arbor festooned with sweet-scented climbers such as honeysuckle and roses. This seat is stained gray to simulate weather-bleached oak.

MATERIALS & EQUIPMENT

33 ft (9.9 m) rough-sawn lumber 1 x 5½ in [1 x 6] (25 x 150 mm)

16 ft (2 m) rough-sawn lumber 1½ x 1½ in [2 x 2] (40 x 40 mm)

exterior-grade plywood ½ x 17¾ x 45¾ in (10 x 445 x 1145 mm)

4 wood-turned finials 4 in (100 mm) tall with ½ in (10 mm) dowel

no. 8 screws 2 in (50 mm) and 1½ in (40 mm)

1 quart (1 liter) wood preservative

2½ quarts (2½ liters) gray wood stain

52 small chamomile plants (*Chamaemelum nobile*)

50 quarts (50 liters) potting soil (approximately)

1 Cut six 18 in (450 mm) side panels from the 1 x 6 (25 x 150 mm) lumber and four 18½ in (470 mm) uprights from the 2 x 2 (40 x 40 mm) lumber. Drill holes in each corner of the boards, then attach the side boards to the uprights using 2 in (50 mm) screws. Sand the rough edges. The posts will be 2 in (50 mm) longer once you have all the side panels in place.

2 Cut three 48 in (1200 mm) front panels from the 1 x 6 (25 x 150 mm) lumber. Drill holes in each corner of the boards and screw them to the two side panels. Turn the side panels on their sides when you do this in order to make the whole structure more stable.

3 Cut three 48 in (1200 mm) back panels in the same way as the front panels. Drill holes and screw the three back boards to the two side panels. To do this, turn the whole structure over so it rests on the front panels.

4 Cut two 43½ in (1050 mm) battens and two 15 in (350 mm) battens from the 2 x 2 (40 x 40 mm) lumber. Attach the battens to the upper boards of the front, back, and side panels from the inside using the 1½ in (40 mm) screws. Position the battens 4½ in (110 mm) from the top of the upper boards. The battens will provide a good support for the plywood that will eventually form the chamomile seat.

5 Using a power drill with a 1 in (25 mm) spade bit, drill 15 drainage holes in the pieces of plywood, as shown.

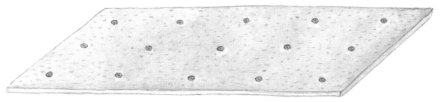

6 Cut a 1¾ x 1¾ in (50 x 50 mm) notch from each corner of the plywood and slide the plywood into position on top of the supports.

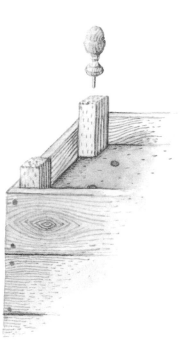

7 Drill a ½ in (10 mm) hole in each of the upright posts and insert the decorative finials. Cover the finished seat with wood preservative and paint it with a gray wood stain.

8 Arrange the plants as shown right, adding moistened potting soil until the plants and the surrounding soil are just below the edge of the seat. Water regularly and clip when uneven.

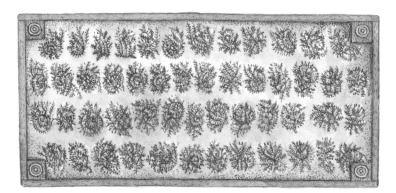

a raised scented window box

This scented window box is best placed below a window, from where the scent
and fragrance of the lavender, rosemary, and thyme can drift into the room.
You can adjust the height of your stand to suit the position of your window.
Choose a window that enjoys a sunny position and keep the plants well
watered, particularly in summer.

MATERIALS & EQUIPMENT

1 plywood window box 8 x 8 x 36 in (200 x 200 x 900 mm)

34 ft (11 m) surfaced softwood ¾ x 1½ in [1 x 2] (25 x 50 mm)

10 ft (3 m) surfaced softwood 1½ x 1½ in [2 x 2] (50 x 50 mm)

galvanized finishing nails 1½ in (40 mm)

no. 8 screws 2 in (50 mm)

waterproof carpenter's glue

1 quart (1 liter) each exterior-grade wood preservative and
exterior-grade latex paint, gray with matt finish

2 strips of ¹/₂₄ in (1 mm) lead, or 26-gauge galvanized sheet metal 3½ x 56½ in (90 x 1450 mm)

2 strips of ¹/₂₄ in (1 mm) lead, or 26-gauge galvanized sheet metal 1½ x 32 in (40 x 800 mm)

galvanized nails ¾ in (20 mm)

potting soil

potted herbs (see page 37)

tin cutters

1 This plywood window box can be bought from a garden center or made at home. If you want to make it yourself, see page 246, where the quantities and measurements of plywood are given.

2 For the molding, start by cutting two side pieces 9½ in (230 mm) long and a front piece 39 in (950 mm) long from the 1 x 2 (25 x 50 mm) lumber. Miter one corner on each short piece and both corners on the long one (see page 247). Fit the molding flush with the top of the box; glue and nail from the inside.

3 To make the stand, start by cutting four 37½ in (950 mm) and four 10 in (250 mm) pieces from the 1 x 2 (25 x 50 mm) lumber. Miter both ends of all the pieces. Glue and nail the joints.

4 Cut four 30 in (750 mm) legs from the 2 x 2 (50 x 50 mm) lumber. Drill holes in the frame corners and screw to the legs. Place one frame ½ in (10 mm) above the top of the legs and another 5 in (130 mm) up from the base.

5 For the lower shelf, cut the following from the 1 x 2 (25 x 50 mm) lumber:
• two 32 in (800 mm) outer slats
• two 36 in (900 mm) inner slats
• three 8 in (200 mm) supports
Position the outer slats flush with the supports and allow the inner slats to protrude by 1½ in (40 mm) at each end. Nail into position.

6 Turn the stand upside down and slide the shelf into the bottom frame. Drill holes for the screws in the shelf supports and screw them to the legs. For added strength, nail into the supports from the outside of the frame. Apply wood preservative to the box, stand, and shelf, and then paint with two coats of latex.

7 Mark a line down the center of one 56½ in (1450 mm) lead strip. Mark two 9½ in (250 mm) long sections at the sides. Divide the side sections into three equal parts and the central section into 10 equal parts. Draw the scallops between these marks so that the top of each scallop meets the bottom edge of the lead. Cut out the pattern with tin cutters. Repeat for the second strip.

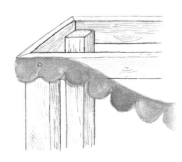

8 Attach one strip to each frame using the ¾ in (20 mm) nails. Put the straight edge flush with the top edge on one side, fold to the front, and use the hammer to form the corners, making them smooth. Nail the second strip to the part of the frame along the shelf.

9 Cut V-shaped notches into the ends of the last two lead strips. Fold over 6 in (150 mm) at each end and bend the central section into a semicircle. Mold to create the wavy effect. Mark three fixing points 1 in (25 mm) below the top molding: one in the center and two 2 in (50 mm) in from the ends. Nail the ribbons to the box, overlapping them where they meet.

Lavender
(*Lavandula angustifolia* 'Hidcote')

Rosemary
(*Rosmarinus officinalis*)

Lavender
(*Lavandula angustifolia* 'Hidcote')

Lavender
(*Lavandula* 'Sawyers')

Silver thyme
(*Thymus vulgaris* 'Silver Posie')

10 Fill the base of the trough with moistened potting soil. Take the plants out of their pots and position according to the planting plan shown above. Work soil around the plants until the soil sits 1 in (25 mm) below the rim of the trough, then water thoroughly. The lower shelf can be used to display a row of painted pots of fragrant herbs that complement those in the window box.

balcony herb boxes

A roof garden, balcony, or other small town garden provides a perfect opportunity to grow herbs. These elegant boxes can be filled with herbs to create a gold, silver, and purple display. You may wish to combine ornamental herbs with those for culinary use. Either follow the planting plans shown here or devise your own herbal color scheme. These boxes have the advantage of looking decorative both from inside the house and from below.

MATERIALS & EQUIPMENT

4 window boxes 9½ x 7 x 36 in (200 x 200 x 900 mm)

61 in (1530 mm) surfaced softwood ¾ x 1½ in [1 x 2] (25 x 50 mm) for molding (optional)

1 quart (1 liter) each exterior-grade wood preservative, dark gray primer,
and dark green gloss paint

metal vise

hammer or mallet

8 galvanized roofing ties 24 in (600 mm) long

24 roofing bolts 1½ in (40 mm) long with ¼ in (6 mm) diameter

45 quarts (45 liters) potting soil (approximately)

2 plastic pots 5 in (130 mm) in diameter

potted herbs (see page 41)

1   The window boxes in this project can be bought at a garden center. (To make them yourself, see page 246, where exact quantities of wood are given.) Unless the lumber has been pressure-treated, coat each box with wood preservative. Apply a layer of primer followed by a layer of dark green gloss paint.

2   You can also add two 9 in (230 mm) moldings and one 38 in (965 mm) molding cut from ¾ x 1½ in [1 x 2] (25 x 50 mm) lumber. Cut two 11 in (275 mm) pieces and one 39 in (975 mm) piece. See step 2 of the instructions for the window box on page 36 for attaching the molding to the box.

3   The brackets are made from galvanized roofing ties to fit the dimensions of the balcony rail, which in this case measures 2 x 5 in (50 x 130 mm). Mark two 8 in (200 mm) sections, one 5 in (130 mm) section and one 3 in (80 mm) section on each tie.

4   Bend the bracket into the correct sections in the metal vise, as shown, and use the hammer to create right angles. The brackets should fit the balcony rail snugly to make the boxes secure.

5   Paint the brackets with dark gray primer and then with gloss paint. Drill three ¼ in (6 mm) diameter holes in each bracket and bolt the brackets to the outside of the box, securing them from the inside. To make sure the boxes fit back to back along the balcony rail, attach the brackets 4 in (100 mm) in from the ends of two of the boxes and 6 in (150 mm) in from the ends of the other two.

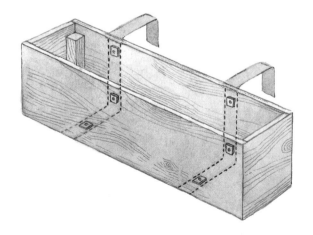

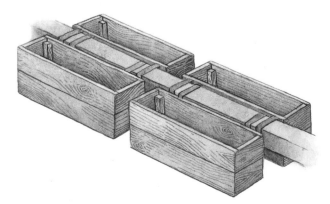

6   Hook the brackets over the balcony rail. The illustration on the left shows how the brackets on the boxes have been deliberately staggered to achieve a snug fit.

7   Fill the balcony boxes with moistened potting soil so that the rootball of
each herb sits 1 in (25 mm) below the top of the box. Plant the herbs according
to the four illustrations below. Plant the herbs in the larger pots first, adding
more potting soil if necessary. Keep the mints, which are invasive, in their
plastic nursery pots.

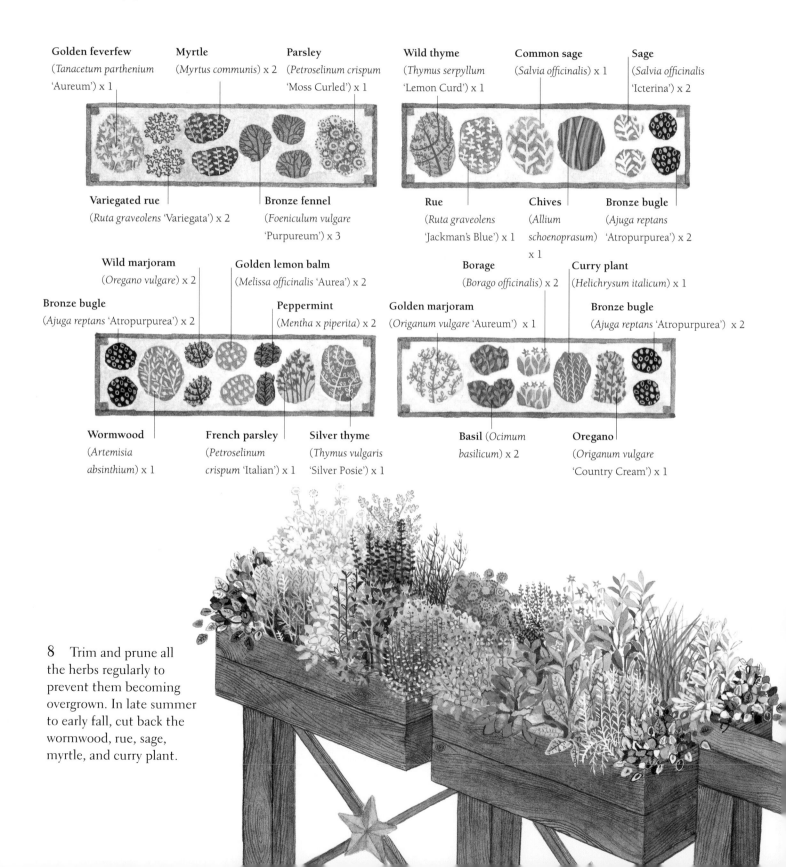

Golden feverfew
(*Tanacetum parthenium*
'Aureum') x 1

Myrtle
(*Myrtus communis*) x 2

Parsley
(*Petroselinum crispum*
'Moss Curled') x 1

Variegated rue
(*Ruta graveolens* 'Variegata') x 2

Bronze fennel
(*Foeniculum vulgare*
'Purpureum') x 3

Wild thyme
(*Thymus serpyllum*
'Lemon Curd') x 1

Common sage
(*Salvia officinalis*) x 1

Sage
(*Salvia officinalis*
'Icterina') x 2

Rue
(*Ruta graveolens*
'Jackman's Blue') x 1

Chives
(*Allium
schoenoprasum*)
x 1

Bronze bugle
(*Ajuga reptans*
'Atropurpurea') x 2

Wild marjoram
(*Oregano vulgare*) x 2

Golden lemon balm
(*Melissa officinalis* 'Aurea') x 2

Bronze bugle
(*Ajuga reptans* 'Atropurpurea') x 2

Peppermint
(*Mentha x piperita*) x 2

Borage
(*Borago officinalis*) x 2

Curry plant
(*Helichrysum italicum*) x 1

Golden marjoram
(*Origanum vulgare* 'Aureum') x 1

Bronze bugle
(*Ajuga reptans* 'Atropurpurea') x 2

Wormwood
(*Artemisia
absinthium*) x 1

French parsley
(*Petroselinum
crispum* 'Italian') x 1

Silver thyme
(*Thymus vulgaris*
'Silver Posie') x 1

Basil (*Ocimum
basilicum*) x 2

Oregano
(*Origanum vulgare*
'Country Cream') x 1

8   Trim and prune all
the herbs regularly to
prevent them becoming
overgrown. In late summer
to early fall, cut back the
wormwood, rue, sage,
myrtle, and curry plant.

galvanized buckets

Hanging galvanized buckets on "S" hooks is an inexpensive and attractive way of displaying plants. A bright and vibrant arrangement, such as the one used here, adds a splash of color, decoration, and movement to a blank expanse of wall in a simple setting. Choose similar flowers in sharp colors and bold shapes to contrast with the plain outline and shiny silver-gray surface of the buckets. For quick results, buy plants instead of starting from seed.

MATERIALS & EQUIPMENT

3 galvanized buckets 12 in (300 mm) in diameter

3 substantial galvanized angle brackets with tops 8½ in (220 mm) long and sides 10 in (250 mm) long

3 eye bolts with nuts to fit the holes in the angle brackets

3 "S" hooks 3 in (80 mm) long

no. 10 screws 2 in (50 mm)

pot shards

15 quarts (15 liters) potting soil (approximately)

4 African marigolds (*Tagetes erecta*)

2 pot marigolds (*Calendula officinalis*)

2 *Artemisia* 'Powys Castle'

2 marguerites (*Argyranthemum frutescens*)

2 black-eyed Susans (*Rudbeckia hirta*)

1 To prepare the buckets for planting, drill three drainage holes in the base of each one.

2 Line the bottom of each bucket with a layer of pot shards 1 in (25 mm) thick.

3 Fill the buckets about two-thirds of the way up with moistened potting soil. Place four de-potted plants in each, making sure that the rootball is 1 in (25 mm) below the top edge of the bucket. Fill in with soil around the edges, lightly covering the surface of the rootballs, and pack the soil. Give the plants a good soaking.

4 The plants used in this project need plenty of sun, so make sure your display area is in a sunny spot—a south-facing wall is ideal. Mark the position of each bracket on the wall with a pencil. In the example shown, the brackets have been staggered up a wall to allow enough space for plants to spread.

To attach the brackets to a stone wall, follow step 5.
To attach the brackets to wood, follow step 6.

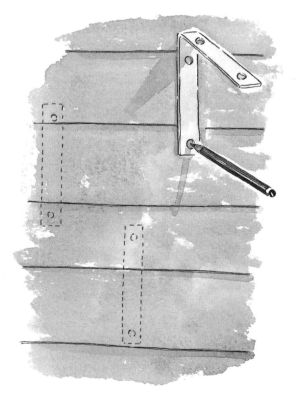

5 Use a power drill, a masonry bit, and special masonry screws to attach the brackets to brick or stone.

6 For wood surfaces use no. 10 screws. If possible, attach the screws into a stud.

7 Put the eye bolt through the end hole on the bracket and secure it with a nut; the height of the buckets can be altered by adjusting the position of the nut. Insert the end of an "S" hook into the eye of the bolt.

8 This bucket has been planted with marguerites and black-eyed Susans. It is especially important to keep all the plants well watered because the containers dry out quickly. Check daily if possible.

alternative planting plan
Bring a burst of sunshine to a bare wall by filling your buckets with dwarf sunflowers (*Helianthus*), *Coreopsis tinctoria*, and *Gazania* 'Orange Beauty.'

decorated containers

a shell-faced trough

A simple decorative treatment refines the look of a concrete garden trough. Aluminum leaf adds a shiny surface to the shells but any metal leaf works well—the most extravagant-looking option being gold. Blue tones have been chosen for the planting arrangement since they complement the silvery-gray of the trough and shells. If you pick your own display, try to stick to one color—a mixture may detract from the decorative impact of the container.

MATERIALS & EQUIPMENT

plain concrete (hypertufa) trough 10 x 24 in (250 x 600 mm)

5 large scallop shells

1 quart (1 liter) dark gray primer

5 sheets metal leaf (with adhesive)

paintbrush

two-part epoxy glue

30 quarts (30 liters) potting soil (approximately)

pot shards

pot-grown plants in 3–4 in (80–100 mm) pots, as follows:

5 *Delphinium belladonna* 'Wendy'

3 cherry-pie heliotropes (*Heliotropium peruvianum* 'Royal Marine')

5 *Laurentia axillaris* 'Blue Star'

5 *Aptenia cordifolia* 'Variegata'

1 Paint the four sides of the trough and the first 1 in (25 mm) inside the top edge with the primer.

2 Pick five large scallop shells of roughly the same size; these can be purchased at a fish market or a craft store. Clean and dry them thoroughly before applying the treatment. Paint the convex side with a single coat of primer.

3 When the primer on the shells has dried, apply the adhesive for the metal leaf (follow manufacturer's instructions).

4 Apply the transfer leaf over the tacky surface of a shell. Test that the adhesive is ready by placing a corner of the transfer onto the shell; if it instantly adheres, the shell is ready to take the leaf.

5 Attach the leaf to the rest of the shell and rub it down lightly with cotton wool. To achieve a distressed appearance, adhere the leaf to the raised areas of the shell; to do this, stretch the transfer over the upper surface and rub the top ridges only so that when you remove the backing the leaf has not stuck in the indents. Repeat this treatment for all five shells.

6 Mark the positions for the shells on the front and sides of the trough with a colored pencil or a strip of masking tape; make your mark where the center of the shell will sit. Site one shell centrally on each side of the trough and three spaced equidistantly on the front panel.

7 The trough and shells are now ready to be joined together. Mix the epoxy glue. Using the applicator or a small wooden spatula, apply generous blobs of the glue to the inside edges of the shells in four or five places, as shown.

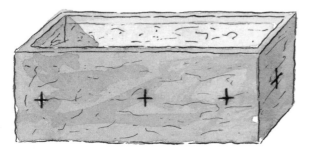

8 Tip the trough onto its side so that the front face is pointing up. Press each shell onto the three marked positions along the top and remove any excess glue spilling out from the sides with a clean applicator.

9 When the glue has dried, turn the trough back onto its base and affix the side shells; hold these in position while the glue sets.

10 Put the trough in a sunny location and plant it in June, using the plan on the left as a guide. The plants have been placed in rows and staggered to fit. The delphiniums are along the back, followed by the laurentias; the heliotropes and the aptenias are at the front.

11 Cover the drainage holes with pot shards. Take the plants out of their pots and tease out the roots. Add moistened potting soil until the plants and the surrounding soil are about 1 in (25 mm) from the trough's rim.

alternative planting plans
For spring, plant *Convolvulus sabatius* with *Vinca minor* 'Alba Variegata'; in winter, fill the trough with winter-flowering pansies.

a lead-faced trough

Lead patinates to a beautiful silvery-gray color—an effect that is simple and quick to achieve. You can simulate the appearance of a lead container by fixing sheet lead to a wooden framework. Take care over size and placement; a window box must sit within the frame and be secured on brackets. Before embarking on this project, ensure that this style of container is in sympathy with the character and architecture of your building.

MATERIALS & EQUIPMENT

wooden box 8 x 8 x 36 in (230 x 230 x 950 mm)

2 pieces softwood ¾ x 1½ x 9½ in [1 x 2] (20 x 40 x 285 mm)

1 piece softwood ¾ x 1½ x 39 in [1 x 2] (20 x 40 x 1030 mm)

no. 8 screws 1½ in (40 mm)

galvanized nails ¾ in (20 mm)

1 quart (1 liter) exterior-grade wood preservative and 1 bottle white vinegar

2 sheets of ¹⁄₂₄ in (1 mm) lead (or 26-gauge galvanized sheet metal),
one 8 x 52 in (250 x 1430 mm) and the other 5 x 58 in (130 x 1550 mm)

6 *Senecio cineraria*

5 *Petunia* 'Ruby'

4 *Osteospermum* 'Whirly Gig'

3 pink bellflowers (*Campanula carpatica*)

3 *Nemesia caerulea*

3 Persian violets (*Exacum affine*)

1 Treat the box inside and out with wood preservative. Wear gloves and and wash your hands when handling the lead, and cut it with tin cutters.

2 Attach the wider strip of lead to one side of the box, top and bottom, with the galvanized nails.

3 Wrap the lead around to the front and use a mallet to achieve a sharp corner.

4 Nail the front in place, top and bottom, at 5–6 in (130–150 mm) intervals. Use the mallet on the other corner and nail the remaining side in place.

5 Take the three sections of softwood and miter one corner on the short pieces and both corners on the longer one (see page 247). Fit the sections together to form the molding around the front and sides of the box, flush with the top edge. Drill holes for the screws around this edge and screw the molding in place from the inside.

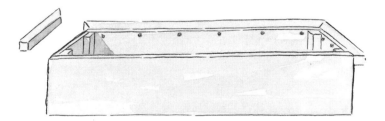

6 Take the second strip of lead and score a line along its length, using a nail and straight edge, 2¼ in (60 mm) down from the top. Divide the bottom into 31 sections of 2 in (50 mm), then divide the scored line into sections of the same size but starting 1 in (25 mm) in from the short end.

7 Join up the marks to form a zigzag pattern, then cut it out using tin cutters.

8 Place the straight edge of the cutout along the inner edge of the box on the side. Nail it in place. To attach the strip neatly around the corner, cut out a 90° notch from the lead, making sure the corner point lines up exactly with the corner of the molding. Hammer down the zigzag edge on the side and wrap the lead to the front of the box.

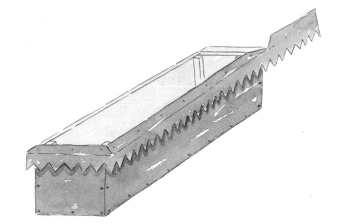

9 Use a mallet to achieve sharp corners and so that the zigzag sits neatly along the outside of the molding. Nail in place. Complete the lead facing for the last side, following the method already used.

10 To give the box a patina, apply white vinegar to the surface of the lead using a damp cloth. Keep applying until a mottled whitish-gray effect appears.

11 If your windowsill slopes, make wedges to level the base of the box. Secure by screwing the inside of the box to the window frame, or use ready-made window-box brackets.

12 Line the box with pot shards and moistened potting soil. Add the plants, matching the colors and numbers listed on page 52 with the plan below. Fill in with potting soil to 1 in (25 mm) below the top, pack it down, and water well.

a rustic window box

The fashion for making objects covered in barked wood started in the
18th century. This design is based on the style of the English Regency
landscape gardener Humphrey Repton, who imitated the forms
of classical architecture using rustic materials such as barked
columns and pine-cone festoons.

MATERIALS & EQUIPMENT

exterior-grade plywood and surfaced softwood (see step 1, page 58)

1 quart (1 liter) each clear wood preservative and green wood stain

14 ft (4 m) halved barked poles with 2–2½ in (50–65 mm) diameter

3 large and 8 small pine cones

no. 8 screws 1½ in (40 mm)

galvanized clout nails 3 in (80 mm)

finishing nails 2 and 2½ in (50 and 65 mm)

pot shards

30 quarts (30 liters) peat-based compost

3 male ferns (*Dryopteris filix-mas*)

6 crested female ferns (*Athyrium filix-femina cristatum*)

9 white cup flowers (*Nierembergia*)

small bag of sphagnum moss

1　Cut the following in exterior-grade plywood:
• 2 pieces for front and back ¾ x 10 x 36 in
  (20 x 250 x 900 mm)
• 2 pieces for sides ¾ x 6½ x 10 in (20 x 160 x 250 mm)
• 1 piece for base ¾ x 8 x 36 in (20 x 200 x 900 mm)

Cut the following in surfaced softwood:
• 4 side supports 1½ x 1½ x 10 in [2 x 2] (40 x 40 x 250 mm)
• 2 base supports 1½ x 1½ x 31½ in (40 x 40 x 810 mm)

2　Drill holes for screws in each corner of the side pieces and screw the side supports flush with the long edges.

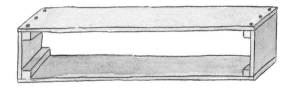

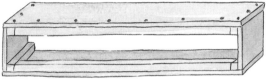

3　Drill holes along the short sides of the front and back pieces and place them flush with the outside edges of the side pieces. Screw into position.

4　Slide the base supports between the side supports, flush with the base, and screw them in place through pre-drilled holes, front and back.

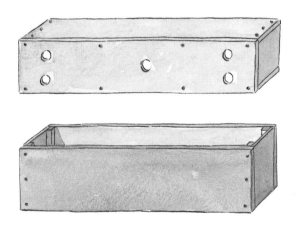

5　Use a power drill with a 1 in (25 mm) spade bit to drill five drainage holes in the base of the box. Then screw it to the bottom of the box, driving the screws into the base supports.

6　Treat the box inside and out with wood preservative. When it has completely dried, apply the green wood stain to the front, back, and sides, on the outside only.

7　To decorate the front of the box, cut four sections of halved barked pole, two 36 in (900 mm) long and two 10 in (250 mm). Miter the ends of all four pieces (see page 247), and use the 2½ in (65 mm) finishing nails to attach them to the front face; drive the nails in at an angle and make sure all the corners meet.

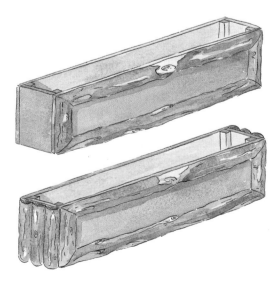

8　For the sides, cut six sections of bark-covered pole, each 10 in (250 mm) long. Using three for each side, position the poles vertically, and nail them into place.

9 With a hacksaw, cut one of the large pine cones in half lengthways; use a vise to do this, or nail one half of the cone to a board, which will hold the cone steady while you cut. With the tip facing down, nail the half-cone to the center of the box with 2 in (50 mm) nails.

10 To complete the festoon effect, cut the small cones in half lengthwise. Use a vise or make a special cutting stand by gluing and nailing two pieces of 1 x 2 in (25 x 50 mm) lumber to a plywood board, placing them to fit the shape of the cone, but leaving a gap at the top to allow for the saw. Push each cone between these rods and secure with nails, then cut in half with a hacksaw.

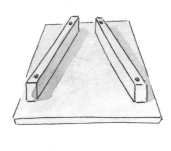

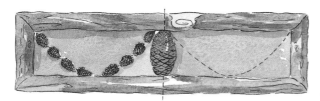

11 Draw two semicircles on the front of the box as a guide for the cone festoon. Glue and nail eight half-cones to each semicircle; start at the top and place matching pairs opposite one another with the tips facing down—if your cones are different sizes, put the largest ones at the top, graduating to the smallest at the central base of the festoon.

12 To construct the pine-cone finials, drill holes in the bottom of the two remaining large cones; make the holes big enough to accept half the length of the finishing nails. Insert the nails and then cut off the heads with a hacksaw.

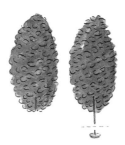

13 The finials are placed in the two side supports at the front of the box. Drill a hole for each and insert; secure them with a dab of waterproof carpenter's glue.

14 Line the base of the box with pot shards and half-fill it with potting soil. Remove the plants from their pots and arrange according to the plan pictured right, with the larger male ferns at the back. Add moistened potting soil to 1 in (25 mm) below the rim, pack down, and fill any gaps with moss. Water thoroughly.

15 Consider carefully where to put the box; ferns need shade and regular watering, although the moss will help retain moisture.

a circular pipe with flowering tree

In a paved garden or where soil is not available, large shrubs or small trees can be grown using inexpensive broad concrete pipes to contain the soil. Here a decorative niche gives height to the arrangement and frames the cascading flowers of the fuchsia.

MATERIALS & EQUIPMENT

1 section of concrete drainage pipe 20 in (500 mm) high with
a 36 in (900 mm) diameter

dark blue-green exterior-grade paint (that can be used on concrete)

50 quarts (50 liters) potting soil (approximately)

slow-release granular fertilizer

pot shards or coarse gravel

1 standard weeping *Fuchsia* x *speciosa* 'La Bianca'

10 lady's mantle (*Alchemilla mollis*)

6 geraniums (*Pelargonium* 'Friesdorf')

1   Choose a concrete drainage pipe to fit the size of the plant. The dimensions given on page 60 are suitable for a small to medium shrub. Conceal the rough surface of the pipe with a fresh coat of paint; dark blue-green harmonizes with most garden schemes.

2   Place the painted pipe in your garden on a level patch of ground. If you plan to use a fuchsia, choose a spot that is relatively shady. Fill the base of the pipe to a depth of 1–2 in (25–50 mm) with pot shards or coarse gravel; this will help improve drainage.

3   If your fuchsia is in a pot, carefully remove it and tease out any enmeshed roots. Fill the base of the pipe with enough potting soil to cover the pot shards and add granular fertilizer. When you have finished planting, all of the plants should be at the depth they were in the pots (see illustration to step 7).

4   Add moistened potting soil to bring the plants and soil to a level about 1½ in (40 mm) below the rim of the pipe.

5   Position the fuchsia in the center of the pipe. Again, the soil surface should be about 1½ in (40 mm) from the top of the pipe.

6 Underplant with lady's mantle and geraniums, and place them around the edge of the container in the positions shown in the illustration.

7 Pack the soil firmly around all the plants and water thoroughly. Monitor the planter for moisture, especially during hot weather.

alternative planting plan
Use two pipes of different diameters to achieve a stepped effect—an idea inspired by medieval garden designs. Plant your tree in the central pipe and fill in the lower level with a seasonal planting scheme. This alternative planting display uses a weeping mulberry (*Morus alba* 'Pendula') above a bed of chamomile (*Anthemis nobile* 'Treneague').

a painted galvanized washtub

A galvanized tin or enamel tub can be turned into an elegant planter by adding ball feet to give it the look of an early-19th-century jardinière. This planter is good for a large mass of colorful annuals and looks attractive either on the ground or raised on a low plinth or wall.

MATERIALS & EQUIPMENT

oval washtub 24 in (600 mm) long and 18 in (450 mm) wide

1 piece exterior-grade plywood ¾ x 14 x 18 in (20 x 350 x 450 mm)

4 wooden balls with 2½ in (65 mm) diameter

4 dowels 2 in (50 mm) long with ⅜ in (7 mm) diameter

waterproof carpenter's glue

1 packet or twelve 2 x 2 in (50 x 50 mm) squares gold leaf (with adhesive)

1 pint (½ liter) each clear wood preservative and dark red primer

1 quart (1 liter) paint (optional)

30 quarts (30 liters) potting soil (approximately)

bag of sphagnum moss

36 dwarf pink and red flowering tobacco plants (*Nicotiana* Domino Series)

1 Begin by making a plywood base to fit in the recessed stand underneath the tub; the ball feet will be attached to this. Place the tub on the plywood and mark the shape of the base on the plywood with a pencil.

2 Draw a second oval about ¼ in (5 mm) inside the first. Cut out the inner shape using a sabersaw.

3 Drill a ⅜ in (7 mm) diameter hole about halfway through each of the wooden balls, making sure it is straight and centered.

4 Dribble a little glue inside these holes and insert the dowels so that they stick out about 1 in (25 mm) above the surface of the balls.

5 Paint the feet with wood preservative. When that has dried, apply two coats of dark red primer to simulate the color of red gesso, which will give the finished effect a warm glow. Sand between each coat.

6 When the primer has completely dried, apply the adhesive for the gold leaf (follow the manufacturer's instructions).

7 Place the gold leaf over the tacky surface of the balls. Smooth over the backing surface before carefully peeling it off, leaving a layer of gold. Continue to apply the gold leaf, overlapping subsequent sheets, until the entire surface of each ball is covered. Rub off excess gold leaf but don't worry if the surface is uneven—this adds to the antique effect.

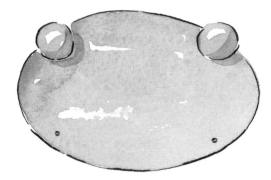

8 Drill four ⅜ in (7 mm) diameter holes into the plywood base to fit the dowels, positioning two at each end of the oval shape, close to the edge. Glue the dowels into the holes, pushing them in until the ball is touching the plywood base.

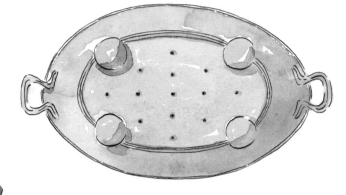

9 Insert the wooden base into the recessed stand of the washtub. Drill a few small holes through the base of the tub and the plywood stand to ensure good drainage.

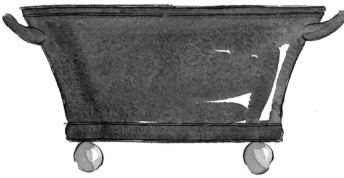

10 If your tub is a suitable color, you may wish to leave it unpainted. However, both enamel and tin can be painted to suit a particular planting plan. Gilding looks best against dark colors; navy-blue latex has been used here.

11 Fill the tub with moistened potting soil to 5 in (130 mm) below the top, forming a slightly dome-shaped surface. Remove the tobacco plants from their pots and arrange them in the tub; for a colorful and dense mound of flowers, mix up the reds and pinks and position the rootballs close together. Fill in the gaps with the remaining soil, firm in, and keep well watered. Place the moss around the plants to help retain moisture and for neatness.

alternative planting plan
Place the tub indoors, in a kitchen or conservatory, or raise it on a low platform and plant with trailing ivy (*Hedera helix*).

terra cotta with a patina

Many modern terra-cotta pots, especially machine-made ones, have a raw,
new look that can detract from the effect of an attractive planting plan. They can
also look out of place next to old containers that have been softened with age.
One answer is to tone down new pots using an antiquing kit that simulates
a patina on terra cotta. Kits can be found at craft stores.

MATERIALS & EQUIPMENT

1 new terra-cotta trough 9 x 9 x 24 in (230 x 230 x 600 mm)

2 terra-cotta pots with a natural patina 10 in (250 mm) in diameter

terra-cotta antiquing kit

small paintbrush

scrub brush

bucket

20 quarts (20 liters) potting soil

pot shards

3 creeping soft grass (*Holcus mollis* 'Albovariegatus') in 6 in (150 mm) diameter pots

2 balls of boxwood (*Buxus sempervirens*) in 1 or 2 gallon (5 or 10 liter) pots

1   Prepare the antiquing kit as directed on the package.

2   Apply the "patina" with a small paintbrush. Take care to paint right into the curves and indents on the relief detail.

3   Once the medium is dry, you can scrub it off using a stiff brush dipped into a bucket of cold water. The object is to leave a white deposit in the relief detail and around all of the edges, but to remove almost all of the paint from the flat surfaces, except for the odd blemish. You need not worry about scrubbing off all the medium because it sinks into the pores of the terra cotta, ensuring that a subtle color change always remains.

4   Cover the bottom of the trough with pot shards. Cover this layer with enough moistened potting soil to raise the top of the grass pots to 1 in (25 mm) below the top edge of the container.

5   Remove the grasses from their pots and place them on the soil layer, then fill the remaining space with soil and pack it down gently. Soak the compost and check frequently to make sure it has not dried out. After eight weeks or so, apply a weak liquid fertilizer. Continue to feed each month in spring, summer, and fall.

6 Line the bases of the 10 in (250 mm) pots with pot shards. Plant the boxwood, filling the pots with firmly packed soil.

7 Display these pots on either side of the trough. The naturally aged appearance of the terra-cotta pots develops only after several years of use out of doors. However, the artificially patinated trough, which has been instantly aged, sits well between them.

alternative effect

An antiqued bronze effect, although more complicated than the patinated trough, is still easy to achieve.

1 Create a glaze by mixing one part water to one part deep blue-green latex paint. Wipe it over the outside of the trough with a rag.

2 Create two more glazes as before with pale blue and pale green latex paint and apply them in random strokes, with a small brush. Dip the brush in water and drag it around the rim, letting the water run down the trough in streaks. Allow to dry. Blend the glazes with fine-grade steel wool.

3 Finally, make a glaze with white latex paint and apply a thin coat to the surface of the trough; while the paint is still wet, wipe it off with a damp cloth, leaving small deposits in the molding and just enough to soften the colors.

71

painted pots

Paint effects can be used to disguise the sometimes rather harsh-looking red appearance of modern terra-cotta pots that have been made by machine. Use the colors chosen here or pick your own combinations to match the architectural background of your garden. To create the greatest impact, paint the pots in simple striking designs and select plants to harmonize with the overall color scheme.

MATERIALS & EQUIPMENT

6 terra-cotta pots: 2 with 9 in (230 mm) diameters;
2 with 7 in (170 mm) diameters; 2 with 6 in (150 mm) diameters

1 quart (1 liter) each yellow latex paint and palm-green latex paint

masking tape 1 in (25 mm) wide

paintbrush and watercolor brush

pot shards

30 quarts (30 liters) general-purpose compost

10 lilies (*Lilium* 'Reinesse')

10 *Osteospermum* 'Buttermilk'

6 lime-and-cream petunias

1   Begin by painting one of each size of pot in green; coat the outside and the top 1½ in (40 mm) on the inside. Repeat for the remaining pots using the yellow paint; you may find that it takes two coats of yellow to hide the terra-cotta coloring underneath. Wait for the paint to dry before applying the pattern.

2   Use the largest pots for the zigzag design. Divide the circumference at the base into five equal parts and mark with a pencil. Then divide the top into five, placing these marks exactly in between the ones already made around the base.

3   Apply the masking tape in strips, joining the top and bottom marks so that a zigzag pattern is formed on the outside of the pots.

4   On the outside, paint the green-based pot yellow, overlapping the edges of the masking tape, and paint the yellow-based pot green. When the paint is completely dry, peel off the tape to reveal a neat zigzag pattern.

5   Select another yellow pot and a green pot and decorate with 1 in (25 mm) spots in the contrasting color using a watercolor brush; draw freehand or make a template by cutting a circle out of a 4 in (100 mm) square of card and painting over it. Finish the pots by painting the top band in the same color as the spots.

6 In this arrangement the other two pots have been left plain, but you can devise any pattern of your choice, remembering that simple bold designs work best. Here are some alternatives.

7 Use the larger pots for the lilies. 'Reinesse' is a stem-rooting lily, so line the pot with pot shards and plant 6–8 in (150–200 mm) deep to allow for root development. A basal-rooting lily such as *Lilium candidum* should be planted 4–6 in (100–150 mm) deep. Plant bulbs from fall to spring, or pot-grown lilies any time. Fill with moistened potting soil to a level of 1½ in (40 mm) from the rim of the pot. Pack the soil and water thoroughly.

8 Line two more pots with pot shards and fill with potting soil so the osteospermums (five per pot) are about 1½ in (40 mm) below the rim of the pot. Pack the soil and water thoroughly.

9 Fill the last two pots with petunias, whose variety makes them ideal for this project. Line the two pots with pot shards and fill with potting soil so the plants (three per pot) are about 1½ in (40 mm) below the rim. Pack the soil and water thoroughly.

brickwork & stone projects

a small brick-edged herb garden

This narrow herb border can be positioned against the wall of a house,
preferably a south-facing wall. It contains basic cooking herbs as well as a selection
of scented herbs. The angled brick edging is a simple way of providing a decorative
divider between the bed and the adjacent gravel path—a technique that was
particularly popular in the 19th century.

MATERIALS & EQUIPMENT

4 wooden stakes

19 ft (5.7 m) mason's line

metal soil tamper

two 80 lb bags ready-to-mix concrete

28 frost-resistant paving bricks (approximately)

coarse gravel

compaction gravel

herbs (see step 6, page 81)

well-rotted organic matter

edging spade • mallet • builder's square

1   Choose a sunny location with good drainage, preferably against a south-facing wall. Measure out a plot 34 x 80 in (850 x 2000 mm) with stakes and mason's line. Use the square to check that the corners are right angles. Remove any turf with a spade and till the soil thoroughly (see Double Digging, page 250).

2   The bricks should be laid in the same direction at a 45° angle around three sides of the plot. Dig a trench around the three sides about 6 in (150 mm) deep and 5 in (130 mm) wide. Compact the earth in the trench—a metal soil tamper will do the job well.

3   Fill the base of the trench about 2½ in (65 mm) deep with concrete and set the bricks into the cement bedding. The bricks do not have to be mortared together.

4   Level the edging by setting up a piece of string 5 in (130 mm) above soil level, all the way around the brick-edged bed. Use a mallet to tap the bricks to the required level, first placing a piece of wood between the brick and hammer to protect the side of the bricks.

5   This bed has been edged by a 3 ft (1 m) wide gravel border. After the edging has set, lay 4 in (100 mm) of coarse gravel and top with a 3 in (75 mm) layer of compaction gravel.

Common sage
(*Salvia officinalis*) x 2

Parsley
(*Petroselinum crispum*
'Moss Curled') x 2

Bronze fennel
(*Foeniculum vulgare*
'Purpureum') x 1

Dill (*Anethum graveolens*) x 1

**English
lavender**
(*Lavandula
angustifolia*) x 1

Garlic chive
(*Allium tuberosum*) x 1

Silver thyme
(*Thymus vulgaris*
'Silver Posie') x 1

Chives
(*Allium
schoenoprasum*)
x 3

Purple sage
(*Salvia officinalis*
Purpurascens
Group) x 1

Creeping thyme
(*Thymus polytrichus*) x 1

Common thyme
(*Thymus vulgaris*) x 1

French tarragon
(*Artemisia
dracunculus*) x 1

Golden marjoram
(*Origanum vulgare* 'Aureum') x 1

6 Plant the herbs in late summer or
spring, and avoid planting when there
is danger of frost. Arrange the plants
according to the illustration above.

a brickwork trough

A tall brick structure creates a stronger visual impact than could be achieved by an urn or a small planter. This trough provides the opportunity for a stunning display of flowering and non-flowering plants, which should nevertheless be simple enough to be appreciated from a distance. The trough can be used for a mixture of permanent structural planting and seasonal annuals—and will act as an important focal point in the garden all year around.

MATERIALS & EQUIPMENT

four 80 lb bags ready-to-mix concrete

three 80 lb bags ready-to-mix mortar

105 SW (frost-resistant) bricks, each 4 x 8 in (100 x 200 mm)

1 piece exterior-grade plywood ½ x 18 x 18 in (10 mm x 450 x 450)

4 concrete blocks (to set height of planting platform)

30 quarts (30 liters) potting soil (approximately)

1 patio tree rose, such as *Rosa* 'Sanders' White Rambler'

1 *Hebe pinguifolia* 'Pagei'

18 tobacco plants (*Nicotiana alata* 'Lime Green')

brick chisel • concave jointer • level • mallet

mason's line • mason's trowel • stakes

1   The trough needs to be built onto 5 in (130 mm) foundations. Excavate a 28 in (700 mm) square hole to this depth. If your trough is to be sited on a gravel path, rake away the gravel from the area before digging the hole.

2   Add water to the ready-to-mix concrete—about two wheelbarrow loads of concrete are needed for the foundations. See Mixing Concrete, page 248.

3   Tip the concrete into the prepared hole, spreading it right into the corners. Level off with a straight-edged board and make sure there are no air pockets; use a level to make sure the surface is horizontal. Leave to dry out for at least 24 hours, and preferably several days, using a plastic sheet to protect it from the weather.

4   Mark out 27 in (680 mm) square with string and pegs, 2½ in (65 mm) above the concrete bed, as a guide for the first course, or layer, of bricks.

5   Add water to the ready-to-mix mortar. Using a mason's trowel, spread a layer of mortar ½ in (10 mm) thick on the concrete slab.

6   Position the bricks as shown. Lay the first course with the "frog" (a small indentation) at the top, spreading all brick ends with mortar. Lay the second layer staggered over the joints on the first. After this and later courses, remove excess mortar from joints.

7   When the mortar is thick enough to hold a thumbprint, run a concave jointer over the joints.

8   Continue to build the container until it has nine layers of brick; make sure the face and height are even by checking at regular intervals with a level.

9 Complete the trough with a coping course, stepping out the brick by 1 in (25 mm). Four filler pieces about 2 x 4 in (50 x 100 mm) are needed to stretch the coping over the edges. (Make odd-sized pieces by scoring the brick all around with a brick chisel and mallet; hit the scored area with increasing intensity until the brick splits.) Fill the inside corners of the step with concrete.

10 To avoid having to fill the entire container with soil, make a stage from the plywood. First drill five 1 in (25 mm) diameter holes in the wood for drainage. Then place the four concrete blocks inside the structure and rest the plywood over them.

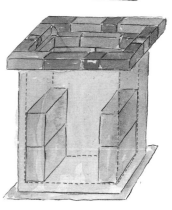

11 For the following planting plan, the hebes and tree rose remain in their plastic pots but are set in soil, whereas the tobacco plants are planted directly into the soil.

12 Place the rose in the center, below the level of the top of the container, then add enough soil to sit the hebes flush with the coping layer. Fill in the spaces with soil, placing the tobacco plants around the rose. Keep the display well watered; use a liquid fertilizer each week.

alternative planting plans
The planting can change with the season. For winter, consider a half-standard holly (*Ilex* x *meserveae* 'Blue Prince') with Kew wintercreeper (*Euonymous fortunei* 'Kewensis'); for fall, try chrysanthemums and flowering kale; for spring, a boxwood cone (*Buxus sempervirens*) surrounded by blue hyacinths.

brick raised beds

Using raised beds in a vegetable garden is a very old tradition that has recently found favor again. The extra depth of good soil allows the plants to put their roots down in search of moisture and nutrition. The beds can easily be reached from all sides so that there is no need to walk on and compact the soil—a big advantage. Start this project in late summer so the prepared beds can remain fallow until spring.

MATERIALS & EQUIPMENT

hardcore

concrete

bricks

good-quality topsoil

well-rotted organic material

seed and plants in variety

level

garden line or pegs and string

Please note: The brick raised beds are slightly more complicated than other projects in this book. Unless you have previous experience with masonry, it is best to consult a professional, using these plans as a guide.

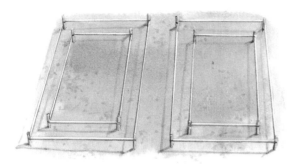

1   The raised beds should be just wide enough so that the center can be reached from either side, and there should be adequate space to move between them. If you live in an area where the ground freezes, consult a professional about how to ensure the stability of your beds.

2   In a sunny but sheltered spot, dig two trenches forming rectangles 6 in (150 mm) longer and wider than the proposed beds. They should be 10 in (250 mm) wide and 16 in (400 mm) deep. Ram down 5 in (130 mm) of hardcore in the base and then pour and level 4 in (100 mm) of concrete on top of this.

3   The walls of the beds are brick; they are easy to construct and look attractive, but they could equally be made of concrete blocks, which are quicker to lay. Build up the walls so that there are two courses below ground and four above—about 12 in (300 mm) higher than the surrounding soil. See note on drainage in step 4.

4   Once the soil in the bed has been dug, water should drain away easily. But to ensure that no water gets trapped within the walls, a vertical joint should be left uncemented every 18 in (450 mm) when laying the course of bricks at ground level.

5   When the concrete has hardened, prepare the bed. Kill or remove all traces of perennial weeds. Dig the soil to at least one spade depth, but preferably double dig it to two, being careful not to bring any subsoil into the top layer. Add plenty of organic material.

6 Once the existing soil in the beds has been cleaned and dug, add a mixture of good-quality topsoil and well-rotted organic material. Fill the beds right up. Do this in fall and leave over winter for it to weather. Top it off with more soil and compost in spring.

7 The area between the beds needs to be kept clear for easy access. To prevent it becoming a mass of weeds or a muddy trail, it can be covered with paving slabs.

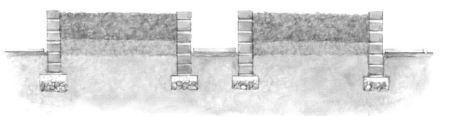

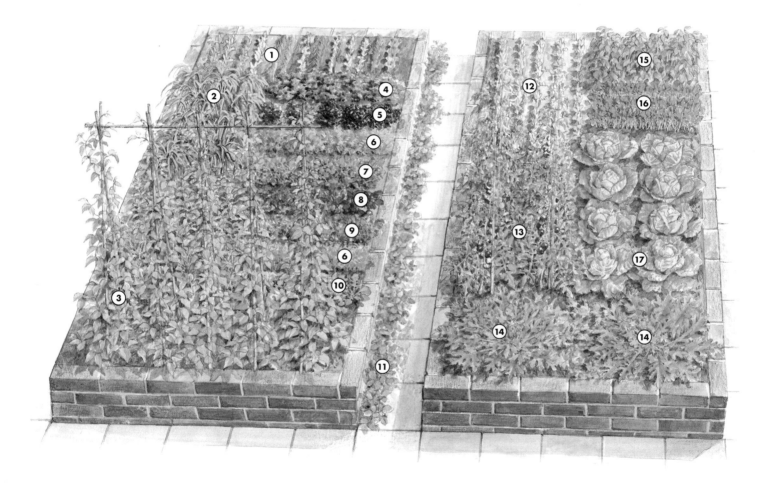

8 Vegetables can be planted in blocks or rows. If you cannot reach directly into the center of the beds, lay a plank between the rows to walk upon. Left in position, planks will also help keep the weeds down and retain moisture.

planting plan

1 Seedlings	6 Carrots	11 Alpine	15 Bush beans
2 Leeks	7 Turnips	strawberries	16 Celery
3 Pole beans	8 Beets	12 Lettuce	17 Cabbages
4 Parsley	9 Parsnips	13 Tomatoes	
5 Lettuce	10 Rutabaga	14 Zucchini	

a raised flower bed

In small paved gardens there may seem to be little choice but to grow plants in pots. However, for a larger display, a generous raised bed is ideal since it holds sufficient soil to sustain a number of plants, both perennials and seasonal annuals. Raised beds also create different levels, which add interest to the space. If they border a path, the extra height can be used to display angular and trailing foliage.

MATERIALS & EQUIPMENT

broken rocks

concrete

pot shards or coarse gravel

bricks, stones, concrete blocks, or pressure-treated 4 x 4 in (100 x 100 mm)
or 6 x 6 in (150 x 150 mm) lumber

landscape fabric

sand

topsoil and well-rotted organic matter

1 *Corylus maxima* 'Purpurea'

4 *Phormium tenax* 'Purpureum'

8 *Heuchera micrantha* var. *diversifolia* 'Palace Purple'

*Please note: The raised flower bed is more complicated than other projects
in the book. Unless you have previous experience with masonry, it is best
to consult a professional, using these plans as a guide.*

1 Choose the material for your flower bed. Brick, stone, concrete blocks, and wood are all possibilities. Wood is perhaps the easiest to use—but be sure to use pressure-treated wood. In general, railroad ties are not ideal because they have been impregnated with creosote. If you live in an area where the ground freezes, you will have to make modifications to ensure the stability of your bed. Consult a local professional for advice.

2 Brick, stone, and concrete blocks are used in the same way. If the bed is not being built on a solid base, dig out a foundation about 10 in (250 mm) deep. A 4 in (100 mm) layer of broken rocks should be rammed into this, topped by a 6 in (150 mm) layer of concrete. The wall is built on top of this.

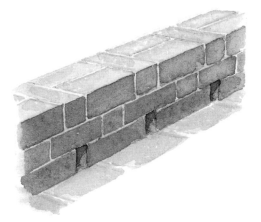

3 It is most important that drainage holes are left in the lower levels of the brickwork to allow excess water to drain. A few gaps in the vertical pointing are usually sufficient.

4 For brick walls, a line of tiles can be added near the top. This detail is not essential, but partly decorative and partly to direct water away from the wall, so that the surface is not stained by repeated drenchings.

5 Add pot shards or coarse gravel to a depth of 3 in (75 mm) or more, then a layer of landscape fabric. Fill with good-quality topsoil, plenty of well-rotted organic matter, and some sand to help drainage. Pack down as you go. Overfill the bed because the soil will settle with time.

6   Plant the bed with flowering plants according to the scheme shown at right, or devise your own scheme. Once filled with soil, raised beds can be treated like any other bed, with the full range of plants that that implies. They allow great scope for the garden designer, but it is essential to plan and build these structures carefully if they are to work well.

planting plan
1 *Corylus maxima* 'Purpurea' x 1
2 *Phormium tenax* 'Purpureum' x 4
3 *Heuchera micrantha* var. *diversifolia* 'Palace Purple' x 8

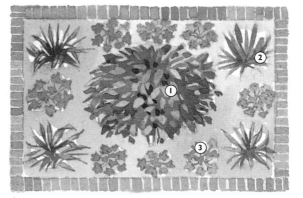

7   Keep the raised bed full of soil and check to make sure the structure is draining efficiently.

alternative materials Pressure-treated lumber is laid directly onto a flat base. Stagger the lumber at the corners for stability. Leave small gaps for drainage.

Slabs of light brown and gray stone are well suited to cottages and country houses. If the house is made of stone, use the local material.

an herb-lined pathway

A brick or paved pathway makes an herb garden accessible even in wet or muddy weather. Paths also articulate and define a design, fulfilling much the same role as dwarf hedges or grass edging. You do not need much space to make this type of pathway. The herb bed included in this project, which measures only 5 x 6 ft (1.5 x 1.8 m), will fit even the tiniest of gardens. The herbs should be allowed to flow informally over the edges of the path.

MATERIALS & EQUIPMENT

4 wooden stakes

23 ft (7 m) string

well-rotted organic matter

1 concrete paver 2 x 2 ft (600 x 600 mm)

9 SW (frost-resistant) bricks

metal soil tamper (optional)

gravel

sand

landscape fabric

5 plastic pots or buckets

1 terra-cotta pot 12 in (300 mm) in diameter

herbs (see page 97)

edging spade • level • square

1   Dig your bed ready for a fall or spring planting, choosing a spot in full sun or part shade. Mark out a 5 x 6 ft (1.5 x 1.8 m) plot with wooden stakes and string, using the square to make sure the corners are right angles. Remove the turf with the edging spade and till the soil thoroughly (see Double Digging, page 250). Amend the soil with well-rotted manure.

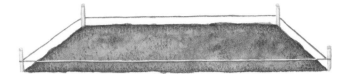

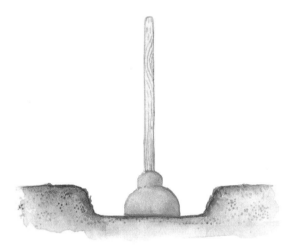

2   The bricks used here are high-fired engineering bricks (although any paving brick is suitable). Their purplish color works well with the purple sage in the planting. To lay the brick paving and concrete paver, dig out an 8 in (200 mm) wide trench to a depth of 6 in (150 mm). Make a 24 in (600 mm) square for the paver. (See opposite for path and paver layout.) Compress the soil in the trench with a soil tamper or use your feet; this will make a solid base for the bricks and the paver.

3   Spread a 4 in (100 mm) layer of gravel in the trench. Top this with landscape fabric. Then spread 2 in (50 mm) of sand. Tamp the sand and spray lightly with water. Gently position the bricks and the paver. Use the level to make sure they are level as you go.

4   Before starting to plant, incorporate some gravel where you plant the thyme, if your soil is not free-draining.

5   Try to buy good-sized herbs that have been grown in 4 in (100 mm) pots; the summer savory and bay can be bought in 6 in (150 mm) pots. Plant the herbs in fall or spring according to the planting plan. Plant the mints in buckets or pots, then sink them into the ground, because mint is invasive. Plant the golden lemon balm in a 12 in (300 mm) clay pot to make a focal point in the center of the bed.

Variegated gingermint
(*Mentha* x *gracilis* 'Variegata') x 3

Wild strawberry
(*Fragaria vesca*) x 2

Golden lemon balm
(*Melissa officinalis* 'Aurea') x 1

Bay
(*Laurus nobilis*) x 1

Golden marjoram
(*Origanum vulgare* 'Aureum') x 2

Variegated gingermint
(*Mentha* x *gracilis* 'Variegata') x 2

Lemon thyme
(*Thymus* x *citriodorus*
'Bertram Anderson') x 4

Wild strawberry
(*Fragaria vesca*) x 2

Summer savory
(*Satureja hortensis*) x 1

Golden marjoram
(*Origanum vulgare* 'Aureum') x 2

Oregano
(*Origanum vulgare*) x 2

Bay
(*Laurus nobilis*) x 1

Summer savory
(*Satureja hortensis*) x 1

Purple sage
(*Salvia officinalis*
Purpurascens Group) x 3

Lemon thyme
(*Thymus* x *citriodorus*
'Bertram Anderson') x 4

6 Trim back the herbs when necessary to prevent them crowding one another. Cut back new growth on the bay in early summer. Cut back the sage before it flowers to achieve a compact shape, and trim the thyme after flowering to encourage bushy growth.

a retaining wall

Slopes in a garden can present problems. One solution is to make a virtue of them by dividing the garden into different levels using retaining walls. These can be planted up in any number of ways, from grass to highly ornamental displays, and so help define different parts of the garden. The surface of the wall can also become a decorative feature in its own right, weathering over time, with trailing plants growing in nooks and crannies.

MATERIALS & EQUIPMENT

for every 8 ft (2.5 m) of wall

concrete

mortar

random-sized stone blocks, about 6 cubic feet (0.1 m^3)

2 terra-cotta drainage pipes

for the bed

coarse gravel or small rocks

good-quality topsoil or well-rotted organic matter

mason's trowel ● wheelbarrow

Please note: The retaining wall is slightly more complicated than other projects in this book. Unless you have previous experience with masonry, it is best to consult a professional, using these plans as a guide.

1 There are several ways of using a retaining wall on a sloping site. The position of the wall will depend on how you want to redefine the area, minimizing the difference in levels (above left) or making a stepped finish (below left). You can use brick, stone, or concrete blocks. A wall that is higher than 18 in (450 mm) should be built by a professional. If you live in an area where the ground freezes, consult a professional about how to ensure the stability of your beds.

2 The finished wall will be 12 in (300 mm) high; like all brick and stone walls, it must have a foundation. If the wall is to support an existing bank, as here, dig away some of the bank to allow you to work. Dig a trench 8 in (200 mm) deep along the line of the wall, three times as wide as the final wall will be. Add a 6 in (150 mm) layer of concrete.

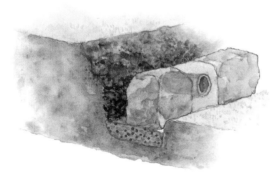

3 Start building the wall. Just above ground level, insert a short length of pipe and secure it in place so that it is in line with the visible base. This will allow water to drain and prevent the bed becoming waterlogged. Add a pipe every 3 ft (1 m). Alternatively, leave spaces between the stones to facilitate drainage.

4 Build above the pipe until the required height is reached. If you plan to include trailing plants in the wall itself, leave a few gaps in the cement-work for planting.

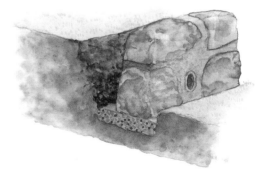

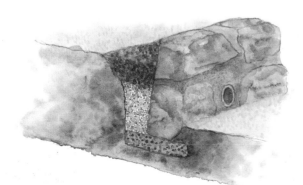

5 To aid drainage, place a layer of coarse gravel or small rocks between the bed and the wall. Backfill with soil rich in organic matter. If you use the soil that was removed from the bank, avoid putting subsoil near the surface.

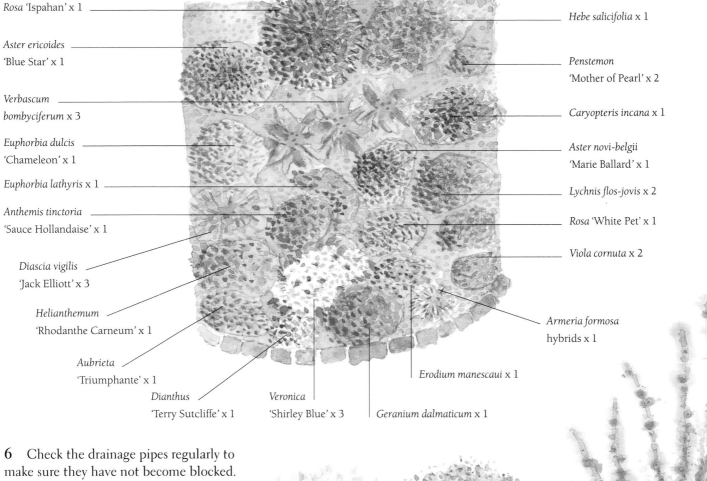

Rosa 'Ispahan' x 1

Aster ericoides
'Blue Star' x 1

Verbascum
bombyciferum x 3

Euphorbia dulcis
'Chameleon' x 1

Euphorbia lathyris x 1

Anthemis tinctoria
'Sauce Hollandaise' x 1

Diascia vigilis
'Jack Elliott' x 3

Helianthemum
'Rhodanthe Carneum' x 1

Aubrieta
'Triumphante' x 1

Dianthus
'Terry Sutcliffe' x 1

Veronica
'Shirley Blue' x 3

Geranium dalmaticum x 1

Erodium manescaui x 1

Armeria formosa
hybrids x 1

Hebe salicifolia x 1

Penstemon
'Mother of Pearl' x 2

Caryopteris incana x 1

Aster novi-belgii
'Marie Ballard' x 1

Lychnis flos-jovis x 2

Rosa 'White Pet' x 1

Viola cornuta x 2

6   Check the drainage pipes regularly to make sure they have not become blocked. Keep wall-growing plants in check with regular clipping. This will encourage bushier growth.

a wall cascade

Walls can be built to incorporate water features ranging from a simple spout to a cascade and pond. In this project the size of the pool and the height of the back wall should be made to suit your site. The slate "steps" are drilled with outlet holes, but a simple hollow is just as effective. If you live in area where the ground freezes, you will have to make modifications to ensure the stability of the walls and the pool; seek professional advice.

MATERIALS & EQUIPMENT

gravel ● concrete

6 x 6 10/10 reinforcing mesh to cover 24 x 72 in (600 x 1800 mm)

5 slabs of slate or cast concrete, slightly concave

bricks

mortar

concrete capstones (about 16) 10 x 12 in (250 x 300 mm)

2 sheets landscape fabric

flexible pond liner

submersible pump and fittings (choose a pump that can handle the volume of the pool and the height of the cascade)

7 ft (2.2 m) length of PVC pipe ½ in (10 mm) in diameter

Please note: The wall cascade is slightly more complicated than other projects in this book. Unless you have previous experience with masonry, it is best to consult a professional, using these plans as a guide.

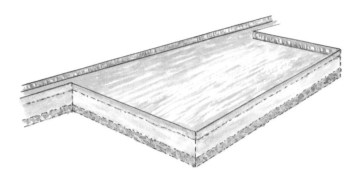

1   After determining the overall size of the feature, dig a 21 in (530 mm) deep trench for the back wall and pool walls. Fill the trench with 6 in (150 mm) of gravel or broken stones and pack it down. Cover with 6 in (150 mm) of concrete and put reinforcing mesh on top of the concrete. Add an extra 6 in (150 mm) of concrete.

2   Build the walls two bricks wide, embedding the PVC pipe for the pump in the back wall. The pipe should run from 4 in (100 mm) above the top of the concrete foundation to the point where the water emerges from the wall onto the top slab.

3   When the pond wall is the desired height, line the pond with two layers of landscape fabric followed by the flexible pond liner. There should be enough liner to overlap the top of the wall by 3 in (80 mm). The concrete capstones will anchor the pond liner (see step 5).

4   Continue to build the back wall and add the slabs at appropriate intervals. Cement the slabs into the wall to a depth equivalent to one row of bricks (below right). The slabs should be slightly concave, carved out by a stonemason if slate is used, or cast into the concrete. Raise one end of each slab by about ½ in (10 mm) to allow the water to run off the other end (above right).

5 Secure the top slab in the back wall just below the end of the pipe so that the water flows directly onto it. Top the pond wall with capstones; these form a decorative finish, provide a surface for plants or for sitting, and, above all, hold the pond liner in place.

6 Install a submersible pump by following the instructions supplied with the unit. Connect it to the lower end of the pipe where it emerges into the pool and run the waterproof cable out over one corner at the back of the pool. Hide the cable under plants.

Please note: Always employ a professional bricklayer to build tall walls if you lack experience, and an electrician to install the pump if you have any doubts.

7 Check periodically that the pump is working effectively, the pipe is clear of debris, and the pond liner is intact and secure.

wood & metal garden structures

a trellis screen

Freestanding trellis is a great boon for the gardener. It allows instant screening from the outside world and is ideal for the creation of "rooms" within a garden. Trellis is perfect for supporting climbing plants in their numerous forms, creating a dense screen of foliage and color. This versatile garden structure can also be incorporated into arches, pergolas, or arbors, providing a foothold for plants while allowing light and air through.

MATERIALS & EQUIPMENT

ready-made lattice panels, usually sold in 4 x 8 ft (1.2 x 2.4 m) sheets

¾ x 1½ in [1 x 2] (20 x 40 mm) lumber for attaching lattice panel to post

pressure-treated posts 4 x 4 in (100 x 100 mm), sized to accommodate the lattice panels and the post hole

post-hole digger

1 finial per post

gravel or prepared concrete for each hole

galvanized nails

plant ties

clematis, honeysuckle, roses, or other climbing plants

level

1 Using a post-hole digger or a shovel, dig a hole for the first post. Put the post in the hole, using a level to make sure it is plumb (vertical). Begin filling the hole with a mixture of gravel and earth. Use a piece of lumber to pack the soil as you go. If your soil is especially loose, you might want to set the post in concrete. If you live in an area where the ground freezes, aim to set your posts 6 in (150 mm) below the frost line. Consult a local professional for advice.

2 Once the main post is solidly in place, nail the first trellis panel to the post. To make the screen more secure, sandwich the lattice panel in 1 x 2 (20 x 40 mm) lumber. Then, attach the framed unit to the posts. Support the far end of the panel at the same time. Align the next post to ensure a neat fit for the trellis and dig the foundation hole.

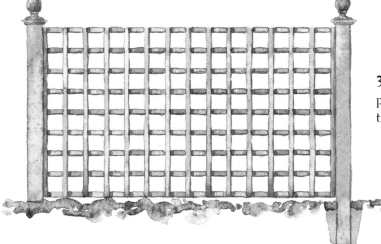

3 Add the gravel base and secure the second post. Making sure it is plumb and square, nail the panel to the post.

4 If you are adding more panels, repeat the process. Once the screen is complete, plant the bed in front.

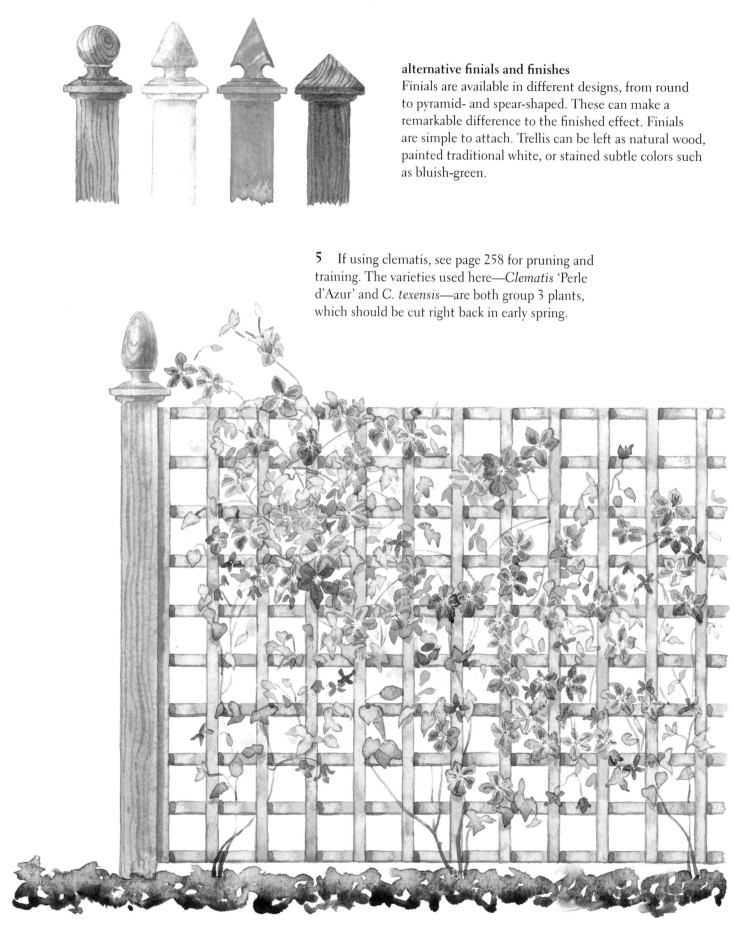

alternative finials and finishes
Finials are available in different designs, from round to pyramid- and spear-shaped. These can make a remarkable difference to the finished effect. Finials are simple to attach. Trellis can be left as natural wood, painted traditional white, or stained subtle colors such as bluish-green.

5 If using clematis, see page 258 for pruning and training. The varieties used here—*Clematis* 'Perle d'Azur' and *C. texensis*—are both group 3 plants, which should be cut right back in early spring.

a rustic trellis

The wood used for this trellis has not been machined, making it pleasingly irregular in thickness and shape. The structure can be covered with plants, but, if a more restrained covering is preferred, rustic trellis is ideal because it is attractive in its own right. The trellis is available ready-made but it is very simple to construct—requiring no advanced carpentry skills—and making your own allows you to tailor the design to your needs.

MATERIALS & EQUIPMENT

4 in (100 mm) galvanized nails

exterior-grade wood preservative

measuring tape

level

plants in variety (see page 115)

for each 6 ft (1.8 m) section of trellis

gravel or prepared concrete for each post hole

uprights: 1 cedar pole 8 ft (2.5 m) long x 4–5 in (100–125 mm)
across (1 pole for each section, plus 1 extra)

crossbars: 2 cedar poles 8 ft (2.5 m) long x 3–4 in (80–100 mm)

struts: 3 cedar poles 3 ft (900 mm) long x 3–4 in (80–100 mm)

1 Secure the upright posts, first stripping the bark from the section that is to be held in the ground and treating it with preservative. Using a post-hole digger or a shovel, dig a hole for the first post, using the technique described in step 1, page 110. Once the upright posts are firm, nail the crossbars to them using simple halved joints (where half the thickness is removed).

2 The most important joints are those where the crossbars meet the upright posts. A simple niche can be cut into the post to correspond with the pointed end of each crossbar. Do not cut too far into the post because this will weaken it. Secure the wood with nails.

3 For the struts, little in the way of true jointing is required. One piece of wood is simply butted up against another and held in place by nails.

4 The struts are useful for training climbers. Measure the poles carefully, make right-angled ends, and nail them securely to the framework.

planting plan

Plants suitable for climbing over rustic trellises include clematis, climbing and rambling roses, honeysuckle, and grape vines. The trellis needs to look balanced, so complementary plants should be selected to grow beneath the structure. This layout, which features two sections of trellis, measures 12 x 4 ft (3.6 x 1.2 m).

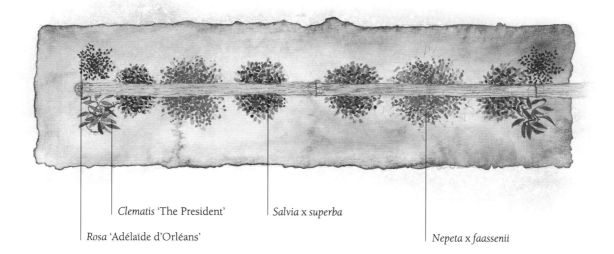

Clematis 'The President'

Rosa 'Adélaïde d'Orléans'

Salvia x *superba*

Nepeta x *faassenii*

5   If wood preservative is applied to the whole trellis (not just the areas of the main posts that are sunk into the ground), the life of the structure will be extended. In early spring check that the trellis is secure and replace any decayed parts.

6   The clematis is a group 2 plant, so it needs light pruning. Do not prune the rose in the first year. After that, each year remove two or three whole stems after flowering; cut back the remaining stems by a quarter and reduce the side shoots by two-thirds.

a trellis-enclosed herb garden

The effect of the planting in this enclosed garden is informal, with the herbs growing together to form solid mounds contained by more formal boxwood and lavender edging and trellis fences. The garden comprises four beds with repeat planting in opposite beds.

MATERIALS & EQUIPMENT

16 wooden stakes and 110 ft (33.5 m) string

4 trellis corner units (see page 247)

16 precast concrete edging slabs 36 x 6 in (900 x 150 mm)

4 wooden obelisks

14 common boxwood (*Buxus sempervirens*)

14 silver boxwood (*B. sempervirens* 'Elegantissima')

4 pot-grown common boxwood pyramids (*B. sempervirens*)

20 English lavender (*Lavandula angustifolia*)

2 pot-grown standard *Phillyrea angustifolia*

2 pot-grown standard honeysuckles (*Lonicera periclymenum*)

gravel

culinary herbs (see planting plans, page 119)

edging spade • builder's square

1   Using stakes and string, mark out a plot 15 x 15 ft (4.5 x 4.5 m). Use a builder's square to make sure the corners are right angles. Remove the turf with an edging spade and till the soil thoroughly (see Double Digging, page 250). Divide the plot into four beds 6 ft (1.8 m) square with 3 ft (900 mm) between each bed.

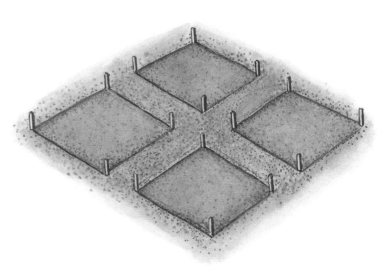

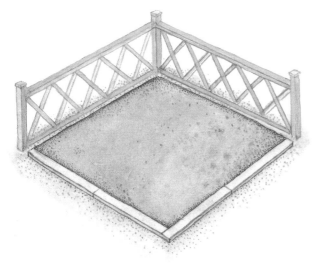

2   Enclose the beds with trellis corner units supported by posts sunk into metal anchors. (Instructions for making the units are given on page 247. A total of 12 posts and 12 post holders will be needed to make four units.) Edge the beds with concrete edging sunk into the ground, as shown, so that 2 in (50 mm) of the edging shows above soil level. Fill the paths between the beds with gravel to allow easy access when harvesting the herbs.

3   Plant seven common box in each bed A every 9 in (230 mm) and five lavender every 10 in (250 mm), as shown. Bed B contains seven silver box and five lavender. Plant a box pyramid in each bed, one standard *Phillyrea angustifolia* in each bed A, and one honeysuckle in each bed B.

Common box
(*Buxus sempervirens*)

Box pyramid
(*Buxus sempervirens*)

Phillyrea angustifolia

English lavender
(*Lavandula angustifolia*)

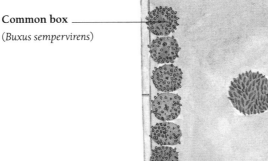

4   Buy pot-grown herbs, preferably in 5 in (130 mm) pots. Plant the herbs in late fall or early spring according to the planting plans for beds A and B shown on page 119, and repeat for the beds diagonally opposite.

5   Cut back the sage, tarragon, and mint in late fall. Trim the rosemary and lavender in mid-spring.

planting plan for bed A

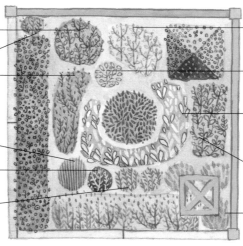

Marjoram
(*Origanum vulgare*) x 1

English lavender
(*Lavandula angustifolia*) x 3

Chives
(*Allium schoenoprasum*) x 1

Rosemary
(*Rosmarinus officinalis*) x 1

Curry plants
(*Helichrysum italicum*) x 2

Greek oregano
(*Origanum onites*) x 1

Sage
(*Salvia officinalis* 'Icterina') x 1

Lamb's ears
(*Stachys byzantina* 'Silver Carpet') x 2

Marjoram
(*Origanum vulgare*) x 1

Echium
(*Echium creticum* 'Blue Bedder') x 3

planting plan for bed B

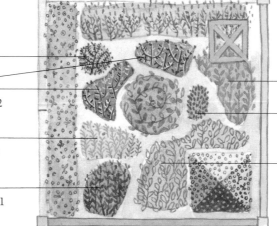

Common thyme
(*Thymus vulgaris*) x 1

Rosemary
(*Rosmarinus officinalis*) x 2

Curry plants
(*Helichrysum italicum*) x 2

French tarragon
(*Artemisia dracunculus*) x 1

Horsemint
(*Mentha x longifolia*) x 1

Winter savory
(*Satureja montana*) x 1

Common sage
(*Salvia officinalis*) x 1

119

vertical planting

A good way to secure privacy in a town garden is to plant vertically. An ordinary hedge is one solution but, even on a roof terrace, more interesting screening effects can be achieved using containers. This project shows how to get a banded effect of pleached linden underplanted with ivy, below which are containers for flowers. If you wish to enclose all the sides of your garden, simply add more troughs and trellis backing.

MATERIALS & EQUIPMENT

2 concrete (hypertufa) troughs 18 x 18 x 24 in (450 x 450 x 600 mm)

1 concrete (hypertufa) trough 18 x 18 x 18 in (450 x 450 x 450 mm)

dark green latex exterior paint

ready-made lattic panels, cut and framed in 1 x 2 in (25 x 50 mm) lumber
to make a unit 6 x 6 ft (1.8 x 1.8 m)

2 pressure-treated posts 1½ x 1½ x 84 in [2 x 2] (40 x 40 x 2200 mm)

coated wire or garden ties • sea-washed pebbles

pot shards • potting soil • slow-release fertilizer

1 red-twigged linden (*Tilia platyphyllos* 'Rubra')

6 ivy plants (*Hedera helix*)

8 white petunias

8 purple *Verbena tenera*

8 white trailing *Verbena tenuisecta* f. *alba*

2 ferns (*Athyrium filix-femina*)

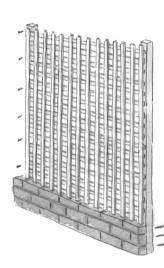

1   Start by securing the trellis backing. In this project vertical posts have been attached to the outside of a 12 in (300 mm) high brick ledge. If you don't have a wall, secure the posts in the ground (see step 1, page 110). Space them 6 ft (1.8 m) apart so that the trellis can be screwed to the face of the posts 12 in (300 mm) above ground level. Alternatively, if you have a high wall or wooden fence, you can train your plants along wires. Stretch plastic or galvanized wire horizontally between vine eyes at suitable intervals and secure with screws.

2   Improve the appearance of the concrete troughs by painting them. Dark colors in a matte finish work best with this planting plan.

3   For the square trough, choose a pot-grown linden with a dense root system and a straight stem, ideally about 6 ft (1.8 m) high with lateral branches at the top; plant in fall or early spring.

4   Cover the drainage holes with pot shards and line with soil. Ease the tree out of its pot and position it toward the back of the trough. Plant the ferns in front of the tree and work soil around the rootballs, making sure they are level. Fill with soil to within 3 in (80 mm) of the top. Finally, add a top dressing of slow-release fertilizer and decorate the surface with pebbles.

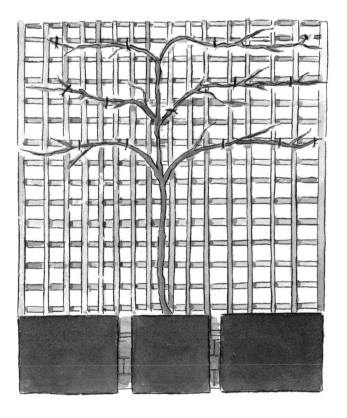

5   For the layered effect at the top of the trellis, three lines of lateral branches have been trained horizontally. Begin by choosing two strong laterals about 4 ft (1.2 m) from the base of the linden, on opposite sides of the stem. Secure them horizontally along the trellis with coated wire. Repeat for the next two lines, spacing them about 12 in (300 mm) apart.

6   Remove all the other side shoots from the stem and grow the trained laterals to the full width of the trellis. Prune annually and cut back excess foliage.

7 Line the larger troughs with pot shards and fill with soil to within 3 in (80 mm) of the top. Choose a plain green ivy with multiple stems that will provide a good hedgelike effect. Position three ivies at the back of each trough and top off with soil. To create a dense screen, train the ivy into a fan shape, tying it to the trellis with coated wire.

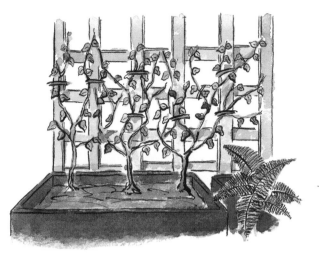

8 Grow the ivy to a height of 3 ft (900 mm) and allow the plants in both troughs to join together. Clip back to keep it flat against the trellis and maintain a straight line along the top; you don't want the ivy to meet the linden, since this would make the layered effect less well defined.

9 Finish off the large troughs with a seasonal planting scheme. White petunias, purple verbenas, and white trailing verbenas have been planted along the front to give a long summer show. Keep them well watered and fed. To make a longer wall screen or enclose a space, add to the number of troughs and secure additional lattice panels.

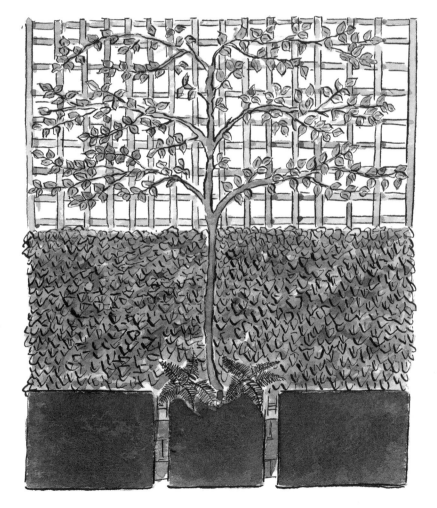

alternative planting plans
Plant forget-me-nots (*Myosotis alpestris*) for a blue haze in spring, or, for fall, plant orange or gold chysanthemums.

a scented arbor

An arbor is the perfect place to sit and relax, especially after a day's work. The scent of the climbers that clothe the arbor and the nature of the structure itself combine to create a soothing effect. The arbor's leafy and flowery walls convey a sense of safe enclosure without being boxed in; it is open and closed at the same time. Here a simple structure is covered with 'New Dawn,' a repeat-flowering rose that produces blooms all summer long.

MATERIALS & EQUIPMENT

ready-made lattice panels, cut to the following sizes and framed
in 1 x 2 in (25 x 50 mm) lumber:

2 side panels at 3 x 6 ft (0.9 x 1.8 m)

1 back panel at 6 x 8 ft (1.8 x 2.5 m)

1 roof panel at 3 x 8 ft (0.9 x 2.5 m)

4 pressure-treated posts 4 x 4 in x 8 ft (100 x 100 mm x 2.5 m)

4 wooden finials

galvanized nails

2 buckets gravel or prepared concrete

plant ties

rustic bench

30 lb (2 buckets) compost

2 *Rosa* 'New Dawn'

level

1 The poles for the back should be placed 8 ft (2.5 m) apart, and the sides 3 ft (0.9 m) apart. See below for instructions on how to determine post depth.

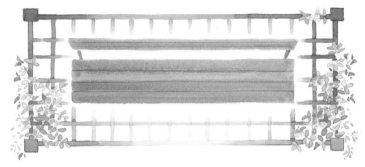

2 Using a post-hole digger or a shovel, dig a hole for the first post. Put the post in the hole, using a level to make sure it is plumb (vertical). Begin filling the hole with a mixture of gravel and earth. Use a piece of lumber to pack the soil as you go. If your soil is especially loose, you might want to set the post in concrete instead.

3 Attach the side and back trellis panels to the posts with galvanized nails. To prevent the wood splitting, drill pilot holes in the panels. Make certain that the panels are level by using a level. Nail or screw the decorative finials to the four posts.

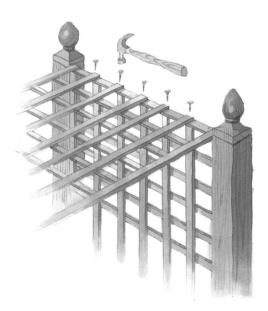

4 Place the roof panel so that it rests on both the side and back trellis panels. Attach the roof by nailing or screwing it directly to the side panels, drilling pilot holes first.

how to determine post depth
Post should be set so that one-third of their length is in the ground. So, a 4 ft (1.2 m) high trellis requires a hole that is 2 ft (0.6 m) deep plus 6 in (30 mm) for a layer of gravel.

Please note: If you live in an area where the ground freezes, aim to set your posts 6 in (150 mm) below the frost line. Consult a local professional for advice.

5   Plant two roses, one at each of the back corners of the arbor. Prepare the ground by incorporating plenty of compost into the soil around the planting area. Dig a hole slightly wider than the rootball of the rose and then plant the rose so the top of the rootball is level with the top of the hole. Fill in with soil. Pack down the earth around the roots and water well. Place the bench in the arbor.

6   Spread the stems of the newly planted roses so that they fan out along the sides and back of the arbor. Tie each shoot with a plant tie or string. As the shoots grow, continue to train them so they eventually cover the whole arbor.

7   Like most climbing or rambling roses, 'New Dawn' is a vigorous plant that produces a profusion of blooms from midsummer to fall. It can even be grown successfully in a partly shaded site.

a wooden obelisk

Trellis obelisks have long been used as a decorative element in the garden. They create an attractive feature on their own, or in pairs frame a view or emphasize a formal approach to a house. The shape of the obelisk makes it suitable for supporting climbers such as ivy, clematis, honeysuckle, or hops. This project uses quick-growing hawthorn; as the hawthorn spreads, use the trellis as a clipping guide to create a tall, elegant pyramid shape.

MATERIALS & EQUIPMENT

rough-sawn lumber (see steps 1, 2, 5, 6, and 13, pages 130–131)

square of exterior-grade plywood ½ x 15 x 15 in (10 x 380 x 380 mm)

no. 8 screws 1½ in (40 mm) and 2 in (50 mm)

galvanized finishing nails 1½ in (40 mm)

1 quart (1 liter) exterior-grade wood preservative

1 quart (1 liter) wood stain

50 quarts (50 liters) potting soil

pot shards

4 hawthorns (*Crataegeus monogyna*)

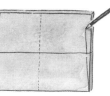

2 Take the two shorter sides and drill holes for 1½ in (40 mm) screws ½ in (10 mm) in from the tapered edges. Cut four corner supports from rough-sawn lumber 1½ x 1½ x 12 in [2 x 2] (40 x 40 x 330 mm), and position flush with the pre-drilled sides and top, leaving a 1 in (25 mm) projection at the bottom. Screw into place.

1 For the short sides: Use two boards ¾ x 5½ x 15 in [1 x 6] (20 x 150 x 390 mm). Lay the boards side by side and draw two lines at the angle shown above. Cut along the lines. Repeat with two more boards, so you have four angled short sides (two of each size). For the long sides: Use two more boards ¾ x 5½ x 17 in [1 x 6] (20 x 150 x 430 mm). Lay the boards side by side and draw two lines at the angle shown above. Cut along the lines. Repeat so you have four angled long sides (two of each size).

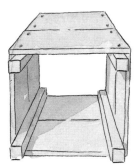

3 Position the longer sides against the outside face of the shorter ones, for a butt joint. Screw in place, making the holes 1 in (25 mm) in from the sides of the longer pieces.

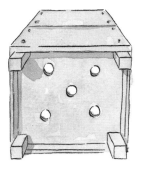

4 For the base, take the piece of plywood and cut a 1½ x 1½ in (40 x 40 mm) square from each corner. Drill five 1 in (25 mm) diameter drainage holes, as shown. Insert the base in position from the bottom of the tub before attaching the four base supports.

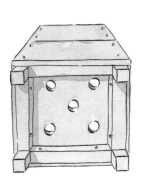

5 Cut four base supports from rough-cut lumber 1½ x 1½ x 12½ in [2 x 2] (40 x 40 x 340 mm) and position flush with the bottom edge of the container on all four sides. Secure with 1½ in (40 mm) screws in pre-drilled holes.

6 For the obelisk, cut the following pieces:
• 4 side supports 1½ x 1½ x 90 in [2 x 2] (40 x 40 x 2350 mm)
• 60 ft (18 m) of lumber 1½ x 1½ [2 x 2] (40 x 40 mm), cut into lengths for rungs
• 1 block 4 x 4 x 4 in (100 x 100 x 100 mm) to form tapered top
• 1 board 1 x 4 x 4 in (25 x 100 x 100 mm) to form base of top

7 Place two side supports 4 in (100 mm) apart at the top and 19 in (480 mm) apart at the bottom. Cut and position one rung 5 in (130 mm) from the top and one 5 in (150 mm) from the bottom—make the rungs slightly longer than the actual width. Nail in place. Mark the positions of 14 rungs between them at 5½ in (140 mm) intervals. Repeat for the opposite side.

8 Cut and nail 14 rungs to the marked positions then cut off all overhangs flush with the side supports.

9 To assemble the obelisk, lay the two completed sections on their sides and cut and nail a top and bottom rung in place across them, positioning as in step 7. Mark the positions of the rest of the rungs as before, then cut and nail them, making sure they line up on all sides. Repeat for the fourth side and cut off the overhangs.

10 For the top, taper the block at an 85° angle. Then cut four 1½ x 1½ in (40 x 40 mm) squares from the corners of the board. Drill holes in the board and screw to the wide base of the top piece with 2 in (50 mm) screws. Slot on top of the main structure and nail to the side supports.

11 Before assembling the whole structure, treat the obelisk and tub with wood preservative. When the surface is dry, apply two coats of wood stain.

12 Line the bottom of the tub with pot shards. Fill the tub with soil and plant the hawthorns. The soil should come within 1 in (25 mm) of the tub's rim.

13 To join the tub and obelisk, first cut four battens 1½ x 1½ x 16 in (40 x 40 x 400 mm). Drill them for 2 in (50 mm) screws and fix two each to opposite sides of the tub; place one flush with the top and the other 5 in (130 mm) below it.

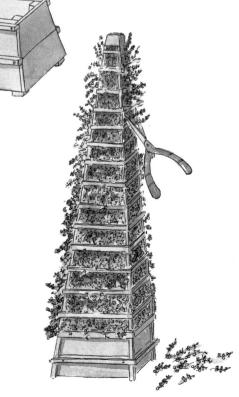

14 Fit the obelisk over the tub, making sure that the structure is square, and screw as above, attaching the bottom two rungs to the battens on the sides of the tub.

15 Make sure the tub is well watered and use a liquid fertilizer during the growing season. Use the trellis as a guide to clipping the hawthorn so that a tall slender green pyramid is achieved. Hawthorn may need clipping several times a year.

miniature hurdles

Decorative edging adds a finishing touch to borders and paths, defining the boundary
between one area and another. An edging can also serve other, practical functions; here, the
charming miniature hurdles, or fences, hold back the plants from the lawn and deter pets
from running into the border. Canes can do the same job but they are far less attractive.
These decorative hurdles are simple to make—an excellent project for the novice carpenter.

MATERIALS & EQUIPMENT

for each hurdle

2 uprights 9 in (230 mm) long and 2 in (50 mm) across

5 crossbars 16 in (400 mm) long and 1 in (25 mm) across

3 braces 8 in (200 mm) long and 1 in (25 mm) across

galvanized nails

exterior-grade wood preservative

chisel

1   These hurdles are made from chestnut but any type of rustic-looking wood will work. Strip off the bark and split the stems in half lengthways with a knife and chisel.

2   Cut the uprights and crossbars to length. Make a pointed end at the bottom of the uprights and drill five holes through each, starting 2 in (50 mm) from the top and spacing them 2 in (50 mm) apart. Shave the ends of the crossbars to fit into the holes.

3   Put the hurdle together and drill small pilot holes horizontally through the uprights and ends of the crossbars. Secure the structure by carefully hammering small galvanized nails through the pilot holes.

4   Cut the central upright bar and the two diagonals to length, position them, drill pilot holes and secure with galvanized nails. The hurdle now has the appearance of a miniature five-bar gate.

5   The secret to using hurdles is to position them before the plants begin to grow. They will restrain excessive growth but some stems and leaves will grow over and through the hurdles, giving them a natural look. Simply push the hurdles into the soil. In packed soil, pilot holes will help.

alternative edging
The simplest form of temporary edging is to make hazel hoops. Use thin, pliable hazel rods about 3 ft (1 m) long, push one end into the soil, and then carefully bend the rod over. Overlap the rods for an elegant, effective finish.

6 Apply an exterior-grade wood preservative that will not harm plants. Periodically check the hurdles for damage and repair or replace any affected parts. Remove the hurdles in the winter, repair any damage, apply a preservative, and store them in a dry place.

a picket fence

A picket fence is the vestige of a defensive barrier in which all the uprights were sharpened to prevent people or animals climbing over. Simple flat or pointed pickets are easy to construct; a sabersaw is useful for more ornate finials. The height of the fence and the distance between the posts is up to you. The rails are usually placed about a quarter of the way from the top and the bottom. The pickets are usually spaced about 3 in (75 mm) apart.

MATERIALS & EQUIPMENT

for each section of fence

gravel or prepared concrete

2 pressure-treated posts 3½ x 3½ in [4 x 4] (100 mm x 100 mm)

pickets ¾ x 2½ in [1 x 3] (20 x 60 mm)

2 rails 1½ x 3½ in [2 x 4] (40 x 100 mm)

galvanized nails

exterior-grade wood preservative, stain, or paint (optional)

level

1 Cut a slight angle on the edge of each rail. Decide on the height of the top rail, and using a chisel or a power drill with a spade bit, carve a rectangular notch in the side of the post. The notch should be ⅛ in (2 mm) wider than the end of the rail, and 1 in (25 mm) deep. Make a similar notch at the location of the lower rail, and make matching notches on the second post. In areas where the ground freezes, set posts 6 in (150 mm) below the frost line. Consult a local professional for advice.

2 Using a post-hole digger or a shovel, dig a hole for the first post. Posts should be set so that one-third of their length is in the ground. So a 4 ft (1.2 m) high fence requires a hole 2 ft (600 mm) deep plus 6 in (150 mm) for a layer of gravel. Put the post in the hole, using a level to make sure it is plumb (vertical).

3 Fill the hole with mixed gravel and earth. Use a piece of lumber to pack the soil as you go. If the soil is very loose, you may prefer to set the post in concrete.

4 Cut the pickets to the desired length. Using a template, cut a pattern on the picket tops. Nail the pickets to the rails.

5 Slide the rails of the picket section into the carved notches on the first post. This will determine the exact location of the hole for the second post. Dig the hole as above; insert the rails into the notches in the second post and secure the picket section to the posts.

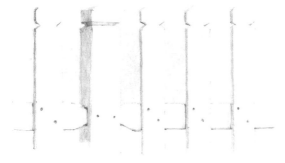

6 Leave the fence as natural wood or treat it with exterior-grade wood preservative, stain, or paint.

to space the pickets evenly
First choose the number of pickets you want between posts. Multiply the number of pickets by the width of a picket to see how much space they will take up. Subtract the answer from the distance between the posts to find out how much leftover space there is. Divide the amount of leftover space by the number of spaces per section, which will be one more than the total number of pickets.

simple and decorative finials

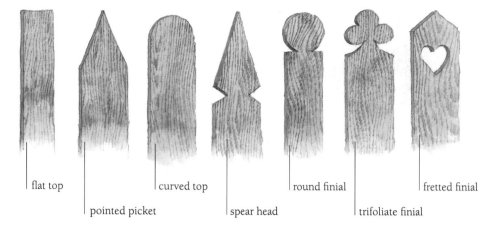

flat top

pointed picket

curved top

spear head

round finial

trifoliate finial

fretted finial

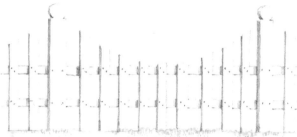

a curved fence

With a little planning, a more elaborate design can be achieved by varying the heights of the pickets and creating a continuous curving finish. The round finials on the posts echo the curve in the picket panels.

a rustic fence

For an informal effect, use natural—but not splintered or coarse—wood, and simply nail all the parts together. Less precise measurements are needed so the job is more straightforward, but there is still room for a decorative pattern in the pickets.

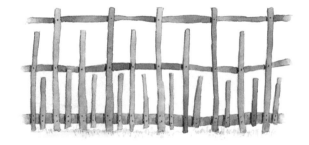

wattle panels

To provide an attractive temporary screen, there is nothing better than wattle panels. They have a rustic appearance that is effective in less formal settings, and they also work well in modern schemes. Their original purpose was to protect and fence in sheep; today, they can keep pets in or out of a particular part of the garden. Wattle hurdles do not last many years but, providing it is not unstable, an aged panel can be picturesque.

MATERIALS & EQUIPMENT

2 posts 6 ft (1.8 m) for the first panel, then 1 per panel

1 wattle panel 6 x 4 ft (1.8 x 1.2 m) for each 6 ft (1.8 m) run

galvanized wire

pliers

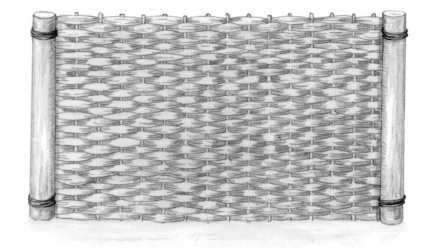

1   To create a long-lasting panel, posts should be secured into the ground. For a temporary screen, the posts can be held firm with rammed earth. Wind galvanized wire around the posts and through the panels 4 in (100 mm) from the top and 4 in (100 mm) from the bottom of the panel.

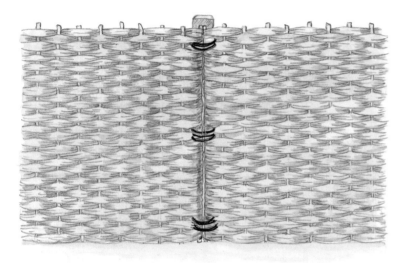

2   Secure the posts as above and bring the edges of the panels together in front of the posts, hiding them. Work the galvanized wire around the post and both panels. Do not leave the end of the wire exposed because this can be dangerous.

3   Untreated wattle panels will last ten years at the most. Treated with a preservative, they will last much longer, but avoid cresote, which can be harmful to plants. In windy situations, use a third length of wire to secure the panels to the posts (above). Check that the posts are secure, particularly where only rammed earth has been used.

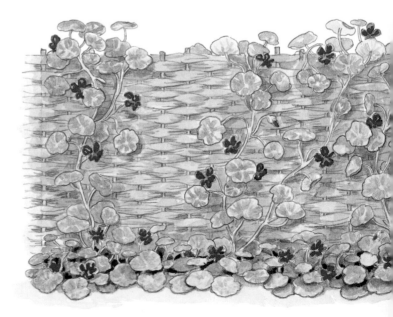

a temporary windbreak

Wattle panels make effective windbreaks while a new hedge is growing. Position them about 3 ft (1 m) away from the young plants so they still get the light. The panels should withstand wind but check them periodically.

a garden screen

Wattle panels can be used as a screen to hide ugly but necessary features such as trash cans and compost heaps. Position the panels so that access is easy and allow plenty of room for maneuver for emptying bins or fetching compost. Use a third wire tie to secure the panels because the structure is likely to be knocked in such a situation.

an open wattle fence

This effective fence is easy to make and is ideal for an internal screen. Hammer stakes into the ground 12 in (300 mm) apart and weave wands of willow or hazel between them. Weave three or four wands in each direction, twisted to form two "ropes."

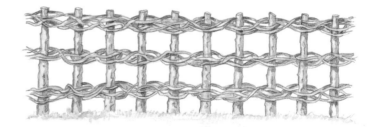

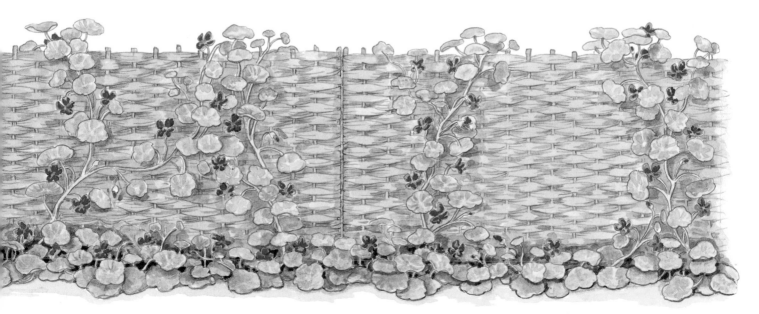

a checkerboard parterre

Achieving a contrast between formality and luxuriant growth is one of
the pleasures of gardening, and this parterre can bring order to an otherwise
informal small garden. The checkerboard effect is based on a design from the
16th and 17th centuries. The herbs are clipped flat and kept square to
accentuate the contrasting colors of the herbs and gravel.

MATERIALS & EQUIPMENT

46 ft (14 m) rough-sawn lumber ¾ x 4½ [1 x 5] (20 x 110 mm)

galvanized nails 2 in (50 mm)

1 quart (1 liter) clear wood preservative

1 quart (1 liter) black wood stain

well-rotted manure

good-quality topsoil

6 squares of landscape fabric 18 x 18 in (450 x 450 mm)

pea gravel

coarse gravel

54 rosemary (*Rosmarinus officinalis*)

1 Cut three 52½ in (1330 mm) and two 70¼ in (1780 mm) boards from the lumber. Cut notches from the boards as shown. The notches should be ¾ in (20 mm) wide and 2½ in (60 mm) deep. Leave a gap of 17 in (430 mm) between each notch.

2 Slot the three 52½ in (1330 mm) inner boards into the notches of the two 70¼ in (1780 mm) inner boards to create the inner framework.

3 Cut two 52½ in (1330 mm) outer boards and two 71¾ in (1823 mm) outer boards from the lumber. Nail these four outer boards to the inner framework using 2 in (50 mm) nails. Unless the lumber has been pressure-treated, coat the parterre with wood preservative.

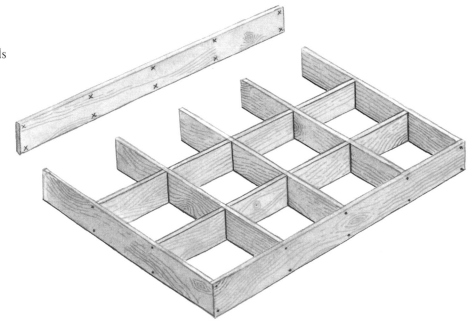

4 Prepare a plot that is about 73 x 54 in (1.8 m x 1.4 m). Remove the soil and create a flat base for the parterre. Plan for 2 in (50 mm) of the parterre to remain above soil level. Treat the wood with preservative, followed by black wood stain. With the parterre in position, add the reserved soil to the planting squares, mixing it with plenty of well-rotted manure and extra topsoil, if necessary.

5   Line those squares that are to contain the pea gravel with the 18 in (450 mm) squares of landscape fabric. Fill each of these squares with the pea gravel to 1 in (25 mm) below the top of the parterre. You can vary the effect by using gravel, marble chips, or colored rock.

6   Remove the rosemary plants from their pots and plant nine in each of the remaining squares, keeping the finished soil level 1 in (25 mm) below the top of the board. You can also use compact, clippable plants such as rue, santolina, or thyme. Clip back the herbs to create the flat, formal effect.

7   The parterre has been surrounded by a band of coarse gravel to act as a textural contrast to the pea gravel in the checkerboard, but it would look equally good set in grass.

herb staging

This raised herb staging—inspired by the 18th-century staging at the
Villa Pisani near Padua, in Italy, where it is used in greenhouses and in an orangery—
makes it possible to grow a large collection of plants in a confined space. Two sections
of the design can be used back to back to make circular staging. The original staging
would have been made from oak, but the plywood used here is far cheaper.

MATERIALS & EQUIPMENT

15 ft (4.5 m) surfaced softwood 2 x 4 in (50 x 100 mm)

exterior-grade plywood ¾ x 24 x 48 in (20 x 600 x 1200 mm)

sabersaw

no. 8 screws 2 in (50 mm) and 4 in (100 mm)

1 quart (1 liter) exterior-grade wood preservative

1 quart (1 liter) dark green exterior-grade latex paint

9 clay pots 6 in (150 mm) in diameter and 8 clay pots 8 in (200 mm) in diameter

potting soil

pot shards

culinary herbs (see page 151)

1   To make the front leg, lay a 39 in (1 m) length of lumber on the ground. Using a long rule as a guide, mark out the angles for the cuts by arranging the rule and lumber to achieve the configuration shown. The final length of the front leg should be 35½ in (860 mm).

2   The configuration of the back legs is as shown. Cut two 36 in (900 mm) pieces of lumber and set on the ground as before. Using the ruler as a guide, mark out the angles for the cuts as shown. Note that the back legs butt onto the front leg; allow for the width of this when marking the angles. The back legs should sit ¾ in (20 mm) down from the top of the ruler.

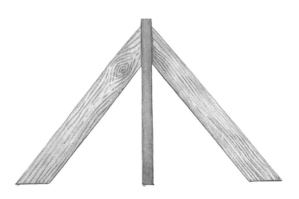

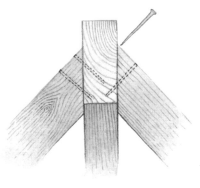

3   Assemble the legs by screwing the two back legs to the front leg using two 4 in (100 mm) screws per leg. Drill the legs as shown. Align the back legs to the front leg ¾ in (20 mm) down from the top of the front leg.

4   Cut nine brackets from the lumber. Position the top shelf brackets first, but cut off a corner from the back leg brackets to a depth of ¾ in (20 mm). Screw the brackets to the legs.

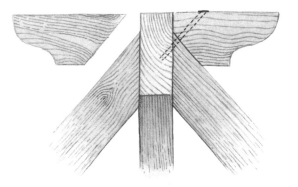

5   Cut out brackets for the middle and lower shelves as before but without cutting off the corners. Position the brackets as shown. On the back legs, from top to bottom, the intervals between the brackets should be 11½ in (290 mm) and 12½ in (320 mm), and the interval between the bottom bracket and the ground should be 10¼ in (260 mm). Drill holes in the brackets and screw to the legs from above. Attach the brackets to the front leg in the same way.

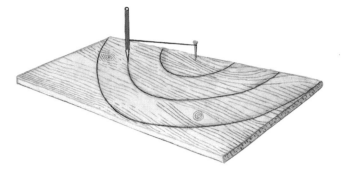

6 To make the shelves, cut from the plywood three concentric semicircles with radiuses of 8 in (200 mm), 16 in (400 mm), and 24 in (600 mm). Mark with a felt-tipped pen attached by string to a nail placed in the center of the long edge of the plywood.

7 Screw the top shelf onto the top brackets from above with three 2 in (50 mm) screws. Attach the lower shelves with two screws per bracket. Unless the wood has been pressure-treated, coat it with wood preservative. Paint with dark green paint.

8 The staging can support nine 6 in (150 mm) pots and eight 8 in (200 mm) pots. Other herbs can be potted up and arranged on the ground. Line each pot with pot shards and pot up the herbs using the potting soil. Leave a gap of ¾ in (20 mm) from soil level to the top of the pot.

upper shelf
Nasturtium (*Tropaeolum* 'Alaska')

middle shelf (left to right)
Wild marjoram (*Origanum vulgare*)
Sage (*Salvia officinalis* 'Icterina')
Marjoram (*Origanum vulgare* 'Gold Tip')

lower shelf (left to right)
Golden marjoram (*Origanum vulgare* 'Aureum')
Rosemary (*Rosmarinus officinalis*)
Curly-leaved parsley (*Petroselinum crispum* 'Moss Curled')
Chives (*Allium schoenoprasum*)
Pineapple mint (*Mentha suaveolens* 'Variegata')
Common sage (*Salvia officinalis*)

ground level (left to right)
Spearmint (*Mentha spicata*)
Purple sage (*Salvia officinalis* Purpurascens Group)
Eau de cologne mint (*Mentha* x *piperita* 'Citratra')
Heartsease (*Viola tricolor*)
Summer savory (*Satureja hortensis*)
Golden lemon thyme (*Thymus* x *citriodorus* 'Aureus')
Spearmint (*Mentha spicata*)

151

a primula theater

This design for a primula theater is for a scaled-down version of an early 19th-century type of shaded staging, made to show off the best examples in a collection and to protect the flowers from sun and rain. It will comfortably hold up to fifteen 4 in (100 mm) pots; terra-cotta pots look best. Paint or stain the theater dark blue, dark green, gray, or black to make a strong background for the rich and varied colors of the primulas.

MATERIALS & EQUIPMENT

surfaced softwood or rough-sawn lumber, and exterior-grade plywood (see over)

1 quart (1 liter) wood preservative or oil-based primer

galvanized finishing nails

waterproof carpenter's glue

exterior-grade latex paint or wood stain

up to 15 terra-cotta pots with 4 in (100 mm) diameters

Primula vulgaris

P. denticulata

P. veris

P. Gold Lace Group

Please note: This project is fairly complex. If you do not have good carpentry skills, you may want to consult a professional.

1 Cut the wood according to the diagrams and measurements.

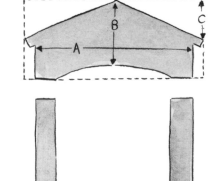

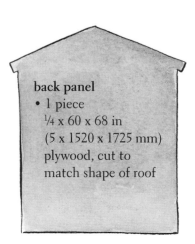

front elevation

- 1 top piece ½ x 22 x 60 in
  (10 x 560 x 1520 mm) plywood
  A: 55 in (1395 mm), B: 21¼ in (540 mm)
  C: 8 in (200 mm)
- 2 pieces 1 x 6 x 43¾ in (25 x 150 x 1110 mm)
  surfaced softwood
- 1 bottom piece 1 x 7 x 43 in
  (25 x 180 x 1095 mm) plywood

back panel
- 1 piece
  ¼ x 60 x 68 in
  (5 x 1520 x 1725 mm)
  plywood, cut to
  match shape of roof

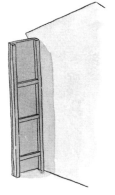

sides and supports
- 2 side panels ½ x 8 x 55 in
  (10 x 200 x 1395 mm) plywood
- 4 side supports 1 x 1 x 55 in
  (25 x 25 x 1395 mm) surfaced softwood
- 6 shelf supports 1 x 1 x 6 in
  (25 x 25 x 150 mm) surfaced softwood

2 To make up the sides, glue and nail the side supports to the outer edges of the two side panels. Then glue and nail the shelf supports 6, 19, and 31 in (150, 480, and 785 mm) from the bottom of the side panels. Glue and nail both completed sides to the plywood back.

3 Construct the frame by attaching the front elevation to the back and sides, gluing and nailing throughout.

4 Cut all the shelves but only attach the bottom one at this stage; sit it on the bottom side supports and glue and nail to the edge of the front elevation.

shelves
- 2 pieces 1 x 6 x 54 in
  (25 x 150 x 1370 mm) surfaced softwood
- 1 bottom piece 1 x 7 x 55 in
  (25 x 180 x 1395 mm) surfaced softwood
  with two 1 x 1 in (25 x 25 mm) notches
  cut from both corners on one long side

5 Secure the roof supports as shown. Wipe off any excess glue. (The actual roof goes on last.)

roof supports
- 6 roof supports 2 x 2 x 8 in
  (50 x 50 x 200 mm)
  surfaced softwood

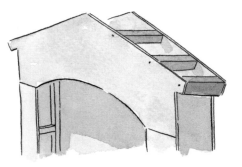

6 Cut out the upper and lower sections of the top pediment from softwood. Secure mitered edges with glue, reinforcing with nails. Glue and nail to the frame in the positions indicated—place the upper section first. (See page 247 for mitering.)

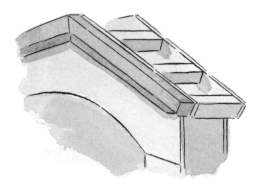

top pediment
- 2 upper sections 2 x 2 in (50 x 50 mm) approximately 30 in (760 mm) long to fit the size of the pediment, mitered at one end
- 2 lower sections 1 x 1 in (25 x 25 mm) approximately 30 in (760 mm) long to fit the size of the pediment, mitered at both ends

7 Using softwood, cut out the base pediment, the capitals, the base column, and the skirting, as highlighted in the diagram, from top to bottom. Secure in the same way as for the top pediment (see step 6).

base pediment
- 1 upper section 2 x 2 x 59 in (50 x 50 x 1495 mm), mitered at both ends
- 2 upper side sections 2 x 2 x 11¼ in (50 x 50 x 280 mm), mitered at one end
- 1 lower section 1 x 1 x 57 in (25 x 25 x 1445 mm), mitered at both ends
- 2 lower side sections 1 x 1 x 10¼ in (25 x 25 x 260 mm), mitered at one end

capitals
All pieces to be mitered at one end.
- 2 pieces 1 x 1 x 9¾ in (25 x 25 x 245 mm)
- 2 pieces 1 x 1 x 8 in (25 x 25 x 200 mm)

base column
All pieces to be mitered at one end.
- 2 pieces ½ x 1 x 9¾ in (10 x 25 x 245 mm)
- 2 pieces ½ x 1 x 7 in (10 x 25 x 180 mm)

skirting
- 1 piece 1 x 7 x 57 in (25 x 180 x 1445 mm), mitered at both ends
- 2 pieces 1 x 7 x 10¼ in (25 x 180 x 260 mm), mitered at one end

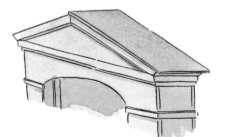

8 Cut out the roof pieces and nail in place, lining up the back edge with the back panel.

- 2 pieces ½ x 12 x 30¾ in (10 x 305 x 780 mm) plywood, mitered at one end

9 Treat the theater and shelves with wood preservative. Finish by painting with an exterior-grade latex paint or stain. Make sure the shelves are totally dry and aired before placing plants, since preservatives and stains are often toxic to plants. Insert the two remaining shelves. Choose your plants from the selection listed. Plant them in shallow terra-cotta pots lined with pot shards and display on the shelves.

a wirework basket

This unusual wire framework is inspired by edgings used in the early 19th century as plant supports. A galvanized-metal strip at the bottom creates a border around a basketlike stand that acts as an attractive frame for rambling rose bushes. The best roses to use for this project are low-growing groundcover types, but you can adapt the basket to accommodate any size of plant, such as larger shrub roses.

MATERIALS & EQUIPMENT

2 pieces galvanized sheet metal 4 x 48 in (100 x 1200 mm)

1 piece galvanized sheet metal 4 x 24 in (100 x 600 mm)
(use a gauge that can be cut with tin cutters)

6 galvanized roofing bolts ½ in (10 mm) long and ¼ in (6 mm) wide

72 ft (22 m) galvanized fencing wire about ³⁄₁₆ in (5 mm) thick

1 piece plywood 1 x 14 x 21 in (25 x 350 x 525 mm)

tin cutters

hacksaw and vise or C-clamp

sabersaw

small pot gray-blue metal primer

roll of thin galvanized wire

well-rotted manure and rose fertilizer

5 bare-root roses such as *Rosa* 'The Fairy'

1   Drill two ⅜ in (7 mm) diameter holes at the ends of each galvanized-metal strip. Then connect the three sections together to form a ring by lining up the holes at the ends and securing the joins with roofing bolts through the prepared holes. This strip acts as a template for preparing the bed and as a retainer for the basket.

2   For the basket, cut the fencing wire into 16 pieces, each 54 in (1360 mm) long; use a hacksaw and vise or C-clamp to hold the wire in place.

3   To shape the wire, you need to make a template from the plywood; this will act as a solid pattern around which to bend your wire. Mark the center point at the top and draw the curved sides to within 8 in (200 mm) of the bottom; this section of the arch remains straight. Cut out the shape with a sabersaw.

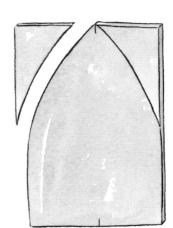

4   Mark the center point on each length of fencing wire. Using a vise, bend the wire at this point into a right angle; it helps to use a mallet as well.

5   Place the right angle over the tip of the template and bend the wire to fit the exact shape of the pattern; the wire should extend for about 4 in (100 mm) beyond the bottom edge of the plywood.

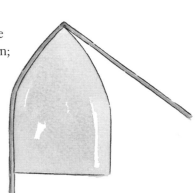

6   Each section of the frame now needs to be bent outward; turn the arches sideways and use the template to guide the curve.

7   Before constructing the basket shape, paint all the metal components with the metal primer; the gray-blue used here looks like a copper patina and provides a good foil for the pink roses.

8   Choose a sunny, flat site for your rose bed. If the area is covered with grass, position the ring and cut around its inner edge to mark the turf. Put the ring to one side and remove the turf by dividing it into squares and lifting out with a spade.

9   Till the bed thoroughly, adding well-rotted manure; gently press the ring in position.

10   Plant the five roses, positioning them as shown. Make sure that the junctions of stem and root are at surface level. Top dress with rose fertilizer.

11   Insert the first arch hard up against the inner edge of the ring with the tip bending out and push it about 6–8 in (150–200 mm) into the ground. Insert the next arch so that it overlaps the original one by half its width. Repeat this process for the remaining arches all the way around the circumference; you may need to readjust the spacing on some of the arches for a neat and even fit.

12   Secure the basket sections together by twisting the galvanized wire around the intersections on each arch.

13   Prune the roses so that they form a slightly domed shape and trim any grass around the outer edge for a formal effect.

alternative planting plans
Try the roses 'White Pet' or 'Nozomi' for a container of this size; for a larger arrangement, use the pink rose 'Marguerite Hilling' or its creamy white sister 'Nevada.' A suitable shrub would be *Camellia japonica* 'Alba Plena.'

a rose arch

Arches can be put to very effective use in the garden, dividing one area from another, but their greatest asset is that they are ideal as supports for growing climbers. Wooden archways are not hard to make from scratch. Alternatively, a variety of elegant metal and wooden frames is readily available in easy-to-assemble kit form, so any garden can be given a passageway and a home for delightful climbers.

MATERIALS & EQUIPMENT

wood or metal garden arch (see page 163)

gravel or concrete (for securing the arch to the ground)

2 *Rosa* 'Adélaïde d'Orléans'

well-rotted manure or compost for each plant

plant ties

level

1 Anchor the arch in a way that suits the materials. A mixture of gravel and earth is usually fine. But, if you have especially loose soil, you might want to anchor the posts in concrete. Many prefabricated arches have their own anchoring system.

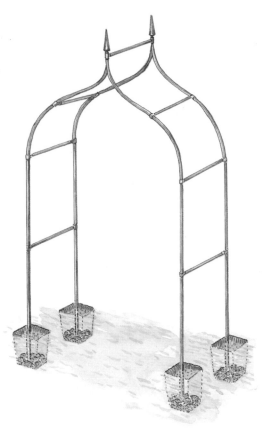

2 Plant a climbing or rambling rose on either side of the outside of the arch, away from any concrete or rammed-earth foundations. The rambler *Rosa* 'Adélaïde d'Orléans' has been chosen here. Lead the stems, with a cane if necessary, onto the arch and tie the branches in.

3 Prune as for climbing roses on a wall (see page 257), but train them up over the arch rather than fanning them out. Tie in any wandering shoots but do not allow the climbers to become too thick. Take care to remove all dead wood.

framing a garden door

marking a rise of steps

arching across a path

alternative uses

Rose arches are used as romantic and fragrant "doorways" from one part of a garden to another, usually covering a path. They can mark a gateway through a wall or a hedge or crown the top of steps, while a series of arches creates a "pergola" effect which can be very dramatic.

selecting an arch

The arch needs to be wide enough to walk through when it is covered with roses. The flowers can extend 12 in (300 mm) into the arch from the sides and the top.

163

decorative planting projects

a scented knot garden

The hedged patterns of knot gardens may have a distinctly medieval feel about them,
but they also have a clear-cut quality that appeals to modern gardeners, especially
if the hedge is scented. Once created, knot gardens are long-lived features and,
although their structure remains the same from one year to the next, their
contents and colors can change with the seasons and with the years.

MATERIALS & EQUIPMENT

5 plant stakes 3 ft (900 mm) long

5 tree ties

sand (on heavy soils)

stakes and string

plants in variety

well-rotted organic matter

1 To make sure you get the scale and proportions right, work out the design on squared paper before planting even a small garden, such as this 14½ x 14½ ft (4 x 4 m) plot. The design can come from your own head or be copied from an historic garden.

The pattern can be geometric or include curved flowing lines, such as those used in paisley designs. The simplest designs are often the most effective; more complicated patterns are best appreciated from above—from an upstairs window, for example.

2 Prepare the ground thoroughly by removing or killing every piece of perennial weed, and dig in plenty of well-rotted organic matter. Santolina, which makes up the hedges, likes a free-draining soil, so dig in sand to improve drainage if necessary.

3 Mark out the location of the santolina hedges using stakes and string. If your design involves curves, first draw a grid over your plan, then lay out a similar grid on the ground with stakes and string. Using the grid as a guide, draw the curves on the ground using a bottle filled with dry sand as a marker.

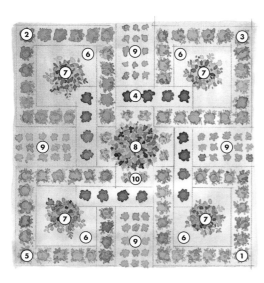

planting plan
1 *Santolina chamaecyparissus* 'Lambrook Silver' x 19
2 *S. pinnata neapolitana* x 19
3 *S. pinnata neapolitana* 'Sulphurea' x 19
4 *S. rosmarinifolia* x 16
5 *S. chamaecyparissus nana* x 19
6 *Viola* 'Jeannie Bellew' x 100
7 *Rosa* 'Fragrant Cloud' (half-standard) x 4
8 *Ilex aquifolium* 'Silver Queen' (standard) x 1
9 *Chamaemelum nobile* 'Treneague' x 60
10 *Nicotiana* 'Domino White' x 8

4 The space within the hedged areas is a mixture of tall perennials surrounded by an ever-changing scene of annuals. Here, roses are underplanted with violas in the four outer squares; nicotiana surrounds a holly standard in the center square; and chamomile lawns fill the open squares.

5 Plant the central holly tree in spring before setting out the hedges. Dig a large hole and work organic matter into the base. Spread out the roots, refill, and water. Secure the tree to a stake using a tree tie about 12 in (300 mm) above ground.

6 Plant the roses, using either bushes or half-standards; the latter need staking in the same way as the holly standard. Plant the santolina at 12 in (300 mm) intervals using the strings as a guide. Water well.

7 In an exposed garden, put up a temporary windbreak of plastic netting until the plants are established. Once established the santolina is quite tough and will withstand even sea breezes.

8 Cut back the santolina in spring. If you dislike its combination of yellow flowers and silver foliage, remove the flower buds before they open.

9 The knot garden may seem full of holes when first planted, but the santolina soon fills out into a thick hedge, which should be kept neatly trimmed. Always remove dead and dying plants: an empty square looks better than one with tatty or dying vegetation.

corner planting

All gardens have odd corners, and since most gardeners complain that they never have enough space, it makes sense to use all these pockets. Another advantage of filling these corners is that it helps to unify the garden and create an overall picture. A common solution is to use bland groundcover plants to fill such areas, but it is far better to create something interesting like this simple, cool-looking border.

PLANTING PLAN

9 *Alchemilla alpina*

4 *Euphorbia stricta*

3 *Mimulus guttatus*

2 *Deschampsia flexuosa*

1 *Geranium pratense* 'Mrs Kendall Clark'

1 *Alchemilla conjuncta*

gravel

1 Rather than filling awkward corners with containers, make a properly prepared bed for your plants. This will need far less work, particularly when it comes to watering. Finish it with gravel, which acts as both a mulch and a complement to many plants, and presents an orderly finish. Gravel can make a highlight of a corner planting, as in this 12 x 12 ft (3.5 x 3.5 m) plot.

2 If you are planting close to a wall, avoid using tall plants that may bend forward, drawn to the light and pushed by winds. Make sure the gravel is well distributed around the plants and that any small rocks are stable.

3 As an alternative to gravel, use concrete pavers and plant between them, creating a tapestry of cover. Erigeron, acaena, thyme, and mint are useful; the last two are also aromatic.

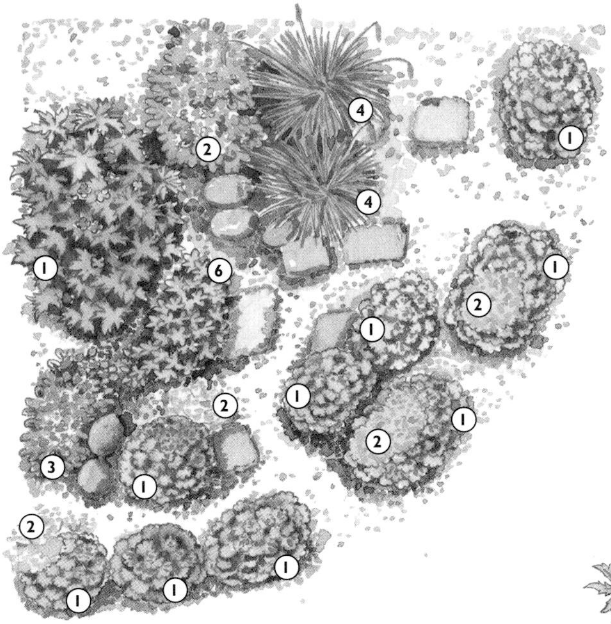

planting plan
1 *Alchemilla alpina* x 9
2 *Euphorbia stricta* x 4
3 *Mimulus guttatus* x 3
4 *Deschampsia flexuosa* x 2
5 *Geranium pratense*
  'Mrs Kendall Clark' x 1
6 *Alchemilla conjuncta* x 1

alternative scheme: a small rock garden

1 A well-built, well-planted rock garden is an excellent solution for many corners, but it needs regular weeding. To make the rock garden secure, and provide a cool, moist rootrun, bury at least half of each rock in the soil. Arrange rocks in tiers, all leaning back slightly.

2 Rock gardens are intended to replicate rocky outcrops, so aim for layers of rocks that are similar in size but not too orderly.

3 When building the garden, never lift more than you can comfortably handle and protect your fingers from crushing stones. Get help if necessary. Move large rocks using a strong pole as a lever or roll rather than lift them. Make sure all rocks are secure.

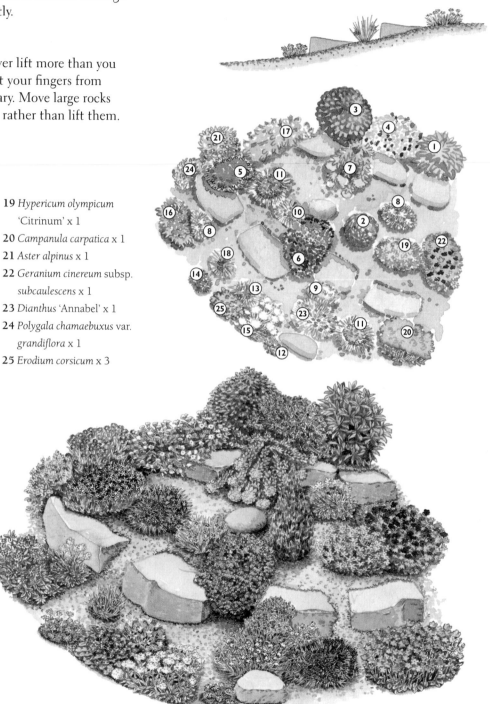

alternative planting plan

1 *Daphne tangutica* x 1

2 *Juniperus communis* 'Compressa' x 1

3 *Picea mariana* 'Nana' x 1

4 *Helianthemum* 'Annabel' x 1

5 *Phlox douglasii* 'Crackerjack' x 1

6 *Aubrieta* 'Joy' x 1

7 *Euphorbia myrsinites* x 1

8 *Lewisia tweedyi* x 2

9 *Erinus alpinus* x 1

10 *Dianthus* 'Little Jock' x 1

11 *Rhodohypoxis baurii* x 2

12 *Armeria juniperifolia* x 1

13 *Pulsatilla vulgaris* x 1

14 *Androsace carnea* subsp. *laggeri* x 1

15 *Achillea clavennae* x 1

16 *Gentiana septemfida* x 1

17 *Convolvulus althaeoides* x 1

18 *Sisyrinchium idahoense* subsp. *bellum* x 1

19 *Hypericum olympicum* 'Citrinum' x 1

20 *Campanula carpatica* x 1

21 *Aster alpinus* x 1

22 *Geranium cinereum* subsp. *subcaulescens* x 1

23 *Dianthus* 'Annabel' x 1

24 *Polygala chamaebuxus* var. *grandiflora* x 1

25 *Erodium corsicum* x 3

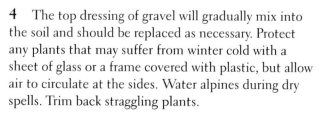

4 The top dressing of gravel will gradually mix into the soil and should be replaced as necessary. Protect any plants that may suffer from winter cold with a sheet of glass or a frame covered with plastic, but allow air to circulate at the sides. Water alpines during dry spells. Trim back straggling plants.

a sweet pea obelisk

The distinctive scent of sweet peas seems to be loved by everyone, probably because it is particularly evocative of childhood. Sweet peas are not just for decorating and perfuming the garden; they also make excellent cut flowers. They are easy to grow from seed and can be used in many decorative ways in the garden, whether you grow them up tripods or allow them to scramble through shrubs with gay abandon.

MATERIALS & EQUIPMENT

seed trays

4 bamboo canes or poles 8 ft (2.5 m) long

garden string

knife

sweet pea seed (*Lathyrus odoratus*)

well-rotted organic material

1   In early spring, sow sweet pea seeds in seed-starting mix in cellular trays. If you use fibrous trays, the resulting seedlings can be planted out without disturbing the roots. Sow one seed per cell, water, and leave in a warm place, out of direct sunlight. Sweet peas can also be bought as seedlings, but growing from seed gives you a much greater choice of colors and scents.

2   When the seedlings have reached 4 in (100 mm), pinch out the tops of the stems just above the nearest set of leaves. If you buy the plants as seedlings, avoid lanky and overcrowded specimens, and look carefully for any evidence of pests and disease.

3   Prepare the ground thoroughly, removing any weeds and adding plenty of organic matter to rejuvenate the soil. Push four canes into the ground (or more for a bigger structure), about 16 in (400 mm) apart, so that their tops meet to form a pyramid. Make certain that each cane is firmly anchored. Tie their tops together in the style of a tepee.

4   Tie string spirally around the obelisk, securing it to each cane as it passes. This is to give the sweet pea plants more to cling to. The string should be strong, but it can be of natural degradable fibers because it only has to last one season.

5 Plant the peas at 8 in (200 mm) intervals around the base of the obelisk. The peas will need to be tied to the canes with string to start with, but will soon be self-supporting. Handle the young stems carefully because they may be brittle. It is wise to put down slug pellets after planting; slugs will eat right through the succulent young pea stems.

6 Sweet peas flower from the summer to early fall, although flowering may be halted by hot weather. "Old-fashioned" varieties produce small but highly scented flowers in blues, reds, pinks, and whites. Newer cultivars are available in most colors; and because they produce larger flowers, they may be more suitable for cutting. Do not let flowers on the plant run to seed—cut them off as they fade.

alternative supports

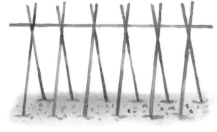

sweet pea wall
A "wall" of sweet peas can be made by arranging the canes as above. Alternatively, sweet peas can be grown up trellising, wire rings, or through shrubs that have flowered in the spring.

container planting
Sweet peas can be grown successfully in containers. They do best in large pots and should be supported with sticks or a tepee of poles. Water the container at least once a day, and twice or more on hot, dry days; apply liquid feed every two weeks. Again, the plants should be deadheaded to encourage flowering.

177

a honeysuckle porch

Honeysuckle is a scent evocative of country lanes, cottage gardens,
and romantic trysts. It is particularly pleasing during the evening,
especially as dusk falls. Possibly the best place to grow honeysuckle
is over a summerhouse or a porch, so that the scent wafts
in through the open door on the evening breeze.

MATERIALS & EQUIPMENT

galvanized wire

screw eyes (plus appropriate mounting hardware, if necessary)

4 wooden blocks (see step 4, page 180)

well-rotted organic matter

peat moss

2 honeysuckles (*Lonicera similis delavayi*)

chipped bark mulch

bamboo canes

plant ties

wire cutters

1   Many houses have a side or front porch, or an attached building, such as a car port or shed. These structures are often additions to a house that add little to its original character. Covering the building with honeysuckle, roses, jasmine, or wisteria will help to disguise its appearance and fill the area with scent. Even attractive porches can be enhanced by having honeysuckle growing over them.

2   Climbing plants such as honeysuckle are best supported by horizontal galvanized wires, firmly anchored to the wall at 18 in (450 mm) intervals. Each wire is secured at its ends by screw eyes anchored into the wall. Bend the wire back on itself, twisting it round with pliers to keep it taut. The wires and screw eyes can be painted the same color as the wall to make them less visible.

3   Honeysuckle will clamber over a roof on its own, but wire supports provide it with better grip in strong winds, especially while it is becoming established. Attach the screw eyes to the eaves on either side of the porch at 18 in (450 mm) intervals and draw the wire taut over the roof.

4   Use blocks of treated wood to lift the wires off the shingles. This gives the honeysuckle more space in which to twine around the wire and protects the roof from damage. The blocks are made by simply nailing together three pieces of wood in a "sandwich." The middle piece should be just a little thicker than the edge of the roof, and should be slightly recessed, so the whole assembly can be slipped over the edges of the roof.

5   Honeysuckle does not like to be dry at the roots, so add plenty of well-rotted organic matter and some peat moss to the soil at the base of the porch. The peat moss fibers hold moisture but allow excess rain to drain away. While digging, make sure all perennial weeds are removed.

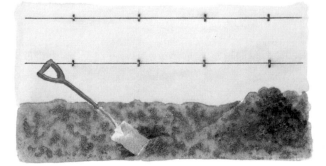

6   Plant one honeysuckle bush on either side of the porch. Dig the planting holes at least 12 in (300 mm) away from the walls. Plant so that the top of the rootball is level with the surface of the soil. Water well and mulch with chipped bark.

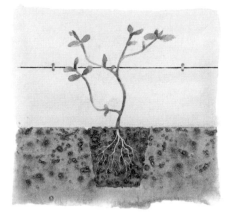

7   Lead the stems towards the wire supports using bamboo canes tipped at an angle from the rootball to the wall. Avoid damaging the roots as you push the canes into the ground. Tie the stems to the cane; when they are larger, tie them directly to the wires.

8   Fan out the shoots so that they cover all the wires. Spread out the shoots at the base of the wall; similarly, spread out any side shoots that emerge farther up the plant, to cover the entire wall. Tie in the shoots with string or plant ties.

9   Honeysuckle need not be pruned at all, but removing dead material helps prevent a build-up of weight as well as making the plant look fresher and neater.

a rose growing through a tree

Scented climbers rambling up through old trees can be a breathtaking sight. Some
of the best climbers for this are the old rambling roses and honeysuckles. Many clematis
species are also suitable, although the fragrant varieties tend to be those with small flowers,
with the exception of the spring-flowering *Clematis montana*. Always choose a strong,
sound tree; never use dead trees because they may break without warning.

MATERIALS & EQUIPMENT

thick rope

rubber padding

plant ties

1 *Rosa* 'Félicité et Perpétue'

two buckets of garden compost

chipped bark mulch

1   When growing a climbing rose up a tree, it is essential to provide support until its questing stems reach the lower tree branches. There are many ways to do this, but one of the most unusual is to use a thick rope. Fasten the rope to one of the main branches, tying it securely but not tightly. Place a sheet of thick rubber between the rope and the branch to protect the bark from chafing. Wrap the rope around the trunk in a loose spiral, allowing room for the trunk to expand without the rope cutting into it. Loosely tie round the bottom of the trunk.

2   Plant the rose about 2 ft (600 mm) from the base of the tree. Dig compost into the soil and plant the rose at the same depth as it was in its pot. If the rose is bare-rooted, plant it to the same depth as it was in the nursery bed (indicated by the soil line on the stem). It is helpful to incline the rose toward the tree, supporting it with a cane during the first months of growth. Water thoroughly and mulch with composted or chipped bark.

3   Train the stems up to the rope and attach with plant ties. As the stems grow, continue to tie in. Inspect regularly to make sure the rope is not constricting or chafing the tree. Cut out any dead wood from the rose, and from time to time remove one or more of the oldest stems to encourage new growth from the base. Tie these new shoots in, either to the rope or to the other stems.

4 Eventually the rose will reach up into the tree and become self-supporting. New shoots from the base will grow up through the increasing mass of stems, and only the more wayward will need tying in. The rope can then be detached or left in place if it is causing the tree no problem. It will take some years before the tree is completely covered—but the wait is worthwhile.

alternative rose supports

fan support
Another way to support a young rose before it reaches the lower branches is to push long bamboo canes into the ground so they extend from the rose into the lower branches.

pole cage
Alternatively, you can place canes around the tree 6 in (150 mm) from the trunk, and train the shoots in a spiral around the "cage." Use hoops of wire to support the canes.

visible trunk
To keep the tree trunk visible, grow the rose up a single pole placed 2 ft (600 mm) from the trunk. Don't attach anything constricting to the tree or drive nails into its trunk.

a scented path

Borders that line paths are always welcome because they bring the viewer close to the plants. This is doubly rewarding with fragrant borders since the sense of smell as well as that of sight is stimulated; in many cases, the action of rubbing against the plants as you pass releases the fragrance. Lavender and rosemary have very distinctive aromas that pervade the air for a long distance, far beyond the pathway.

SCENTED PLANTS TO USE

fragrant foliage	**fragrant flowers**	
Aloysia triphylla	Berberis	Lupinus
Artemisia	Choisya ternata	Matthiola
Lavandula	Convallaria majalis	Nicotiana
Mentha	Daphne	Osmanthus
Monarda didyma	Dianthus	Philadelphus
Myrtus communis	Erysimum	Reseda odorata
Origanum	Hesperis matronalis	Rhododendron (azaleas)
Rosmarinus	Hyacinthus	Rosa
Salvia officinalis	Iris unguicularis	Sarcococca
	Lathyrus odoratus	Syringa
	Lilium	Viburnum
		Viola odorata

1   Fragrant plants add a special dimension to the garden. Many plants, such as lavender, produce the most wonderful perfumes, which are perfect for creating a relaxing atmosphere. Lavender is shown here; more suggestions are given on page 186. This delightful path is 9 x 25 ft (2.5 x 7.5 m).

2   Most garden paths should be wide enough for two people to walk side by side; allow at least 5 ft (1.5 m). Paths that are purely for access can be narrower but should still take a wheelbarrow comfortably. For this scented path there should be adequate room in the beds on either side for the lavenders to grow without overhanging the path too far. As a general rule, borders should be twice as wide as the height of the tallest plants to be used.

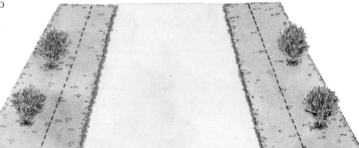

3   Using a string as a guide, plant the lavenders in a straight row, each close enough to the next to merge with its neighbors at maturity, which is about 2 ft (600 mm) all around. To make a consistent picture, use the same variety for all the plants. Seed-grown plants might be cheaper, but the colors can vary. Plant the shrubs to the same depth as they were in their pots, pack down, and water. If possible, mulch the plants to retain moisture and inhibit weeds.

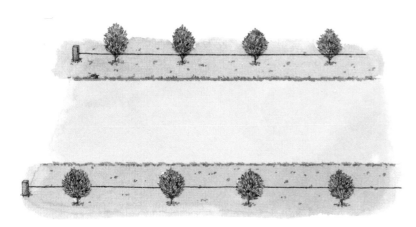

4   Lavender should be sheared in late summer. Remove all flower stems and cut away about 1 in (25 mm) of the previous season's growth. Shape the beds into a slightly undulating low hedge.

alternative pathway
Cottage-style gardens have paths over which everything seems to spill. Paths for this kind of border should be wide enough to accommodate both the spreading plants and the passage of people. Typical fragrant plants for this type of display are border pinks, especially the old-fashioned varieties.

alternative planting plan
1 *Lupinus* 'Kayleigh Ann Savage' x 1
2 Chives x 3
3 *Dianthus* 'Haytor White' x 1
4 Thyme x 1
5 Sage x 1
6 *Dianthus* 'Gran's Favorite' x 2
7 *Artemisia caucasica* x 1
8 *Alchemilla mollis* x 2
9 *Geranium sanguineum* 'Album' x 1
10 Mint x 1
11 *Dianthus* 'Laced Monarch' x 1
12 *Tanacetum parthenium* 'Aureum' x 1

189

herb topiary

Woody-stemmed herbs trained as decorative topiary specimens for containers add formal structure to an established herb bed or act as a focal point beside an entrance or seat. Rosemary is particularly good for training into a half-standard. A native of the Mediterranean, it grows well and looks good in terra cotta. You can also train sweet bay and myrtle into topiary half-standards and herbs such as lavender into small topiary balls.

MATERIALS & EQUIPMENT

1 young pot-grown rosemary (*Rosmarinus officinalis*)

1 terra-cotta pot 11 in (280 mm) in diameter

1 quart (1 liter) potting soil

1 bamboo cane 24 in (600 mm) tall

coated wire or plastic ties

small pruning shears or scissors

1   Choose a rosemary plant with a strong, single leader. Plant in the terra-cotta pot with potting soil. Push the 24 in (600 mm) cane, which marks the final height of the half-standard, into the pot and tie loosely to the single leader using coated wire or plastic ties. Take care not to damage the bark.

2   Cut off all the side shoots using small pruning shears or scissors to direct the plant's energy up the main stem. Leave a sufficient number of shoots at the top of the stem to sustain the plant and to encourage vigorous growth in the crown.

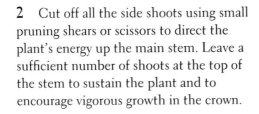

3   In the second year, when the stem of the rosemary has reached the required height of 16 in (400 mm) above the level of the soil, cut out the top of the lead shoot. This cut marks the approximate base of the final crown.

4   Allow several top shoots to develop. Once they have reached a length of 3–4 in (80–100 mm), cut out the end of each top shoot. Keep the main stem clear of any side shoots.

5 During spring and summer, when the new growth occurs, continue to pinch out the ends of the top shoots once they have grown by 3–4 in (80–100 mm), to achieve a dense and shapely head. You can collect the rosemary clippings for use in your home.

6 Each year, start clipping the rosemary standard in mid-spring and trim throughout the growing season in order to keep a tight head. Underplant with pansies (*Viola* x *wittrockiana*) to add further decoration around the edge of the pot.

7 Water regularly and thoroughly, especially if it is sunny or windy. Clip throughout the growing season and remove any leaves from the stem. During the growing season, feed every two weeks with liquid fertilizer. Unless they are frostproof, terra-cotta pots should be brought indoors in winter.

8 In spring transplant pot-bound plants to a larger pot, or top dress with fresh compost, organic matter, and slow-release fertilizer.

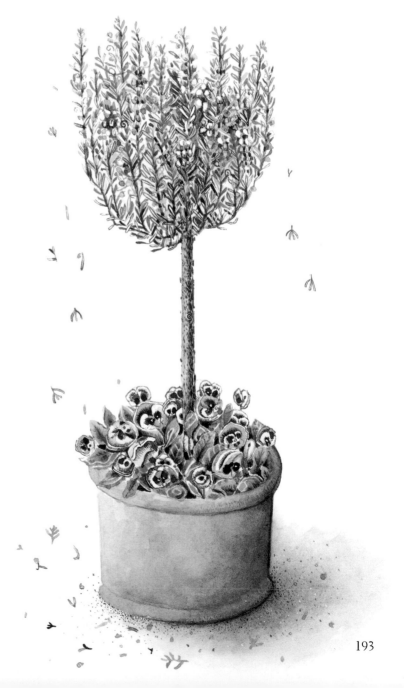

edible planting projects

baskets of tomatoes

In a small garden, every square inch can be exploited to produce vegetables. Vertical space can be filled using hanging baskets and window boxes; and with careful choice of plants, the baskets can be attractive as well as productive. Here tomatoes have been mixed with flowering and foliage plants, but they can be grown alongside other vegetables if space allows. Several baskets in a group, hung at different heights, make an impressive display.

MATERIALS & EQUIPMENT

for each basket

liner

galvanized screw eye and S-hook

potting soil

slow-release fertilizer or liquid fertilizer

1 tomato 'Tumbler'

2 *Petunia* 'Purple'

2 variegated Swedish ivy (*Plectranthus coleoides* 'Variegatus')

utility knife

1   Hanging baskets are available in a range of materials and designs. Wire baskets are inexpensive and light, but wrought iron, terra-cotta, wicker, or wooden baskets may be preferred for aesthetic reasons. Before a basket can be filled and planted, it must be lined.

2   Fit the lining, which may be of fiber, molded paper, moss, or polyethylene; the last is ugly if not completely covered by plants. The lining should be porous, so drainage is not a problem. It is easier to work on the basket if it is supported on a bucket, particularly if a heavier basket is used.

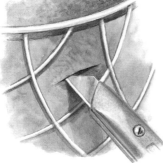

3   Hanging vegetable baskets look their best when completely covered with plants, so plant the sides as well as the top. Use a utility knife to cut holes or slits in the liner before pouring in the compost. Make the holes no bigger than necessary to push the plant through.

4   Fill the basket with soil to just below the level of the slits in the lining. Wrap the roots of the petunias in damp tissue to prevent damage, then push the young plants through the holes in the lining, spreading their roots. Add more soil to fill the basket. Petunias make a decorative display, but productive plants such as lettuces can be substituted.

5   Plant the tomato in the center of the basket, so that it will hang down on all sides. The 'Tumbler' variety has been specially developed for planting in hanging baskets.

6   Baskets with tomatoes should be hung in a warm, sunny position. If there is an existing beam, then a stout eye screwed into the woodwork will be enough support. Be certain that the beam is strong and in good repair. The basket can be hung at any height that seems appropriate. Lower is easier for care and maintenance, but baskets usually look best above eye-level.

7 For ease of watering, use a long-reach watering tool. Unless it is raining, baskets should be watered once a day, twice on hot days. They also need regular feeding. A slow-release fertilizer can be added to the soil at planting time, or use liquid fertilizer every two weeks. Harvest fruit as it ripens and remove any that is damaged or overripe.

8 Vegetable baskets look especially attractive in groups of three or more. Hang them at different heights for the best effect. For variety, hang one basket below another.

alternative planting plan
As an alternative to tomatoes, plant the basket with cut-and-come-again lettuces. There are varieties available with red foliage and with crinkly and oak-leaf-shaped leaves. A surprising number can be included in the basket if planted around the sides as well as on top. The result will be a ball of colorful lettuce.

chile peppers in pots

Pot-grown chile peppers make a spectacular display. There is a wide range of varieties producing yellow, orange, red, or purple fruit on bushes of different sizes. In some cultivars, the chiles hang from the branches; in others they are borne upright. In temperate climates, chiles grow slowly; the first fruits appear about 15 weeks after planting. They start green but redden—and grow hotter—as they ripen.

MATERIALS & EQUIPMENT

seed trays

seed-starting soil

pots for seedlings 3 in (75 mm) in diameter

large terra-cotta pots

pot shards

potting soil

a variety of chile pepper plants or several types of seed

1 Chiles are branching perennials that vary in size and shape according to variety but can grow to a height of 5 ft (1.5 m). Unable to tolerate low temperatures, they must be started off in a greenhouse or conservatory and not be placed outside until the threat of frost has passed. If the temperature drops below 65°F (18°C), the plants should be taken indoors. Sweet peppers, which can tolerate slightly cooler conditions, can be used as a substitute.

2 If you cannot obtain young plants, chiles may be grown from seed, which is more readily available. Sow seed in trays in early to mid-spring and place in a warm spot or propagator at about 70°F (21°C). Don't let the seed dry out. There should be no need to water seed in a propagator.

3 When the plants are large enough to handle, move them out into individual pots and keep them in a warm environment. Avoid placing the pots in a cold draft and beware of frost.

4 Terra-cotta pots are perfect for growing peppers; ideally, use pots that are less than about 18 in (450 mm) across because they are light enough to move inside during cooler weather. The pots must have a hole in the bottom to allow excess water to drain away.

5 Once the plants are about 4 in (100 mm) high, plant them into their final pots. Cover the bottom of each container with pot shards or stones; fill with potting soil and plant the chiles. Water well. If using large pots, place them in their final spot before filling with soil; moist soil adds greatly to the weight.

6 When the plants reach a height of about 6 in (150 mm), pinch off their growing tops to make them bush out. Chile peppers need a sheltered site and should be placed against a south-facing wall, which will radiate heat during the night, helping to keep the plants warm.

7 If the plants you have chosen are about the same height, use some form of staging—such as bricks or inverted pots—to vary the level. This will display the plants to best effect and let light through to the plants at the back. The plants will need watering every day and perhaps twice a day in very hot weather. Use liquid fertilizer every ten days once the fruit has started to swell.

8 The pepper can be picked as soon as it is large enough. It can be picked at the green stage when it will be at its mildest, or at its final colored stage (red, yellow, or purple), when it will be hotter. Pick the pepper with part of the stalk still attached. Be certain to have picked all the peppers, or have moved the plants inside, before the first frost.

a patio container garden

Ordinary terra-cotta pots, strawberry jars, and half-barrels can be used to transform the smallest paved patio into a kitchen garden capable of producing vegetables, fruit, and herbs of the highest quality. A well-designed patio kitchen garden can also be an attractive feature in its own right. Virtually any fruit or vegetable can be grown there, although, for obvious reasons, it is sensible to choose the less rampant varieties.

MATERIALS & EQUIPMENT

variety of terra-cotta pots

potting soil

pot shards

plastic drainpipe 2 x 24 in (50 x 600 mm)

pick ax

plants in variety

1   A paved patio provides many opportunities for planting crops for the table. Conventional terra-cotta pots and strawberry jars are attractive, versatile, and free-draining; larger containers can be made from half-barrels. Spreading plants are best planted directly into the ground: use a pick ax to lift a few of the paving slabs.

2   Remove any gravel and sand from beneath the lifted slabs. Break up the soil below this and fill the remaining space with fresh soil or compost. Plant spreading herbs such as thyme and marjoram, and water well.

3   Most vegetables will grow well in pots, even small containers. Fill the bottom of the container with pot shards and top with potting soil. Sow the seed thinly on the top and cover with a thin layer of compost. Cover the pot with netting to prevent birds or other animals from disturbing the compost.

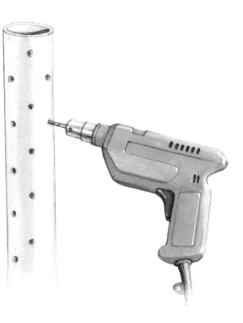

4   There are several types of strawberry pot available; the most decorative are tall terra-cotta towers that have planting holes in the sides as well as on top. Strawberry towers are also available in plastic.

5   Tall strawberry pots are difficult to water right to the bottom, but it is easy to make a simple device to ensure they are well irrigated. Buy a length of 2 in (50 mm) diameter plastic pipe. Drill three ⅛ in (3 mm) holes around the pipe at 2 in (50 mm) intervals along its length.

6 Place the pipe in the center of the pot and fill around it with compost until you reach the first hole in the side of the pot. Ease the strawberry roots through the hole and continue to fill the pot with soil until the next hole is reached. Plant further strawberries until the pot is full.

7 Fill up the pipe with water, and water the top of the pot. If the bottom of the tube is not in tight contact with the bottom of the pot, the water may run out too quickly. If this is the case, slow down its release by ramming a ball of crumpled plastic down the tube. This will slow the flow sufficiently to allow water to percolate out of the side holes. Water the pot regularly so that it never dries out.

8 Water the pots every day and feed with liquid fertilizer once a week. Keep plants neat, removing diseased individuals on sight. Harvest vegetables and fruit as required; avoid leaving overripe and rotting produce on the plants.

planting scheme

1 Lemon balm	6 Carrots	10 Patio rose	15 Potatoes
2 Rosemary	7 Tomatoes	11 Beets	16 Zucchini
3 Lemon verbena	8 Cherry	12 Strawberries	17 Marjoram
4 Runner beans	tomatoes	13 Leeks	18 Pear tree
5 Sage	9 Gooseberries	14 Lettuce	

fruit trees in pots

Fruit is usually associated with large bushes or even huge trees, but most varieties have dwarf forms that grow well in containers; there are even apple trees that can be grown as patio plants. However, it is the more exotic fruit, such as oranges and lemons, that are especially good for using in containers. This is partly because they are easier to look after if they can be moved in and outdoors, but also because they are very decorative.

MATERIALS & EQUIPMENT

terra-cotta pots

pot shards or stones

potting soil

slow-release fertilizer or liquid soil fertilizer

young fruit trees and plants (see page 211)

1   Pots should be considered from a practical as well as aesthetic perspective. Plastic pots are much lighter than terra cotta but are easier to overwater and provide less thermal insulation for a plant's roots in winter. The Mediterranean fruit trees used here look better in terra cotta pots, which are cooler in summer and warmer in winter. Heavier than plastic, they are less likely to fall over in a wind, but they are more difficult to move when full of soil.

2   Spread a layer of pot shards or stones on the bottom of the pot. Partly fill with moistened potting soil; put in the plant and fill up to the top. Pack down and water.

3   While most exotic fruit trees need winter protection, they can be placed outside in summer, preferably against a south-facing wall. This not only provides a good backdrop, but also acts as a storage heater at night. Placing them in a corner offers even better protection. Avoid locations overshadowed by other buildings or trees, or those that funnel drafts over the trees. Containers should be watered every day, and at least twice on hot days or when there is a drying wind. Add a liquid fertilizer to the water once a month.

4   The plants in this arrangement need to be repotted every year into larger pots until they reach their maximum size. Remove them from their existing pots and shake off any loose soil around the rootball. As the plants mature, some of the roots can be trimmed back. Repot into pots one size larger using fresh soil, and water well.

5 In temperate climates, oranges, lemons, and limes can be grown purely as ornamentals, but they will fruit if given enough warmth. To maximize fruiting in cooler areas, the plants, in their pots, should be kept in a greenhouse or solarium to provide them with extra warmth. One or two smaller pots can act as fillers around the edge of the group. Climbers provide an attractive backdrop.

planting plan
1 Calamondin orange
  (*Citrofortunella microcarpa*)
2 Natal plum
  (*Carissa grandiflora*)
3 Meyer's lemon
  (*Citrus meyeri* 'Meyer')
4 Variegated lemon
  (*Citrus limon* 'Variegata')
5 Assorted low-growing
  ornamentals
6 Rosemary
  (*Rosmarinus officinalis*)
7 Wisteria (*Wisteria floribunda*)

6 Most exotic fruit trees and bushes are not winter hardy and so need to be moved under cover—a warm greenhouse or solarium is ideal. The plants should be kept inside until all possible threat of frost has passed and the daytime temperature reaches an average of 68°F (20°C). Be careful not to overwater during the winter—just keep the soil barely moist.

alternative planting plan
Less exotic fruits are hardier and can be left outside as long as their containers do not freeze solid. Protect the containers by wrapping straw or bubble wrap around them when cold weather is forecast. Remove wrapping in warm weather.

1 Pole apple
2 Standard gooseberry
3 Blueberry
4 Strawberry tower
5 Rosemary
6 Assorted low-growing ornamentals

culinary herb half-barrels

These half-barrels are the perfect way to grow a selection of cooking herbs
in even the smallest of gardens, whether you have a small courtyard or simply
a balcony. The planting schemes create attractive displays and provide a source
of fresh produce for the kitchen. Your could also grow other culinary herbs
such as borage, dill, and caraway.

MATERIALS & EQUIPMENT

3 half-barrels, 12 in (300 mm), 19 in (475 mm), and 24 in (600 mm) in diameter

dark gray metal primer

1 quart (1 liter) dark green exterior-grade latex paint

180 quarts (180 liters) potting soil

plastic pots (see pages 214–215)

culinary herbs (see pages 214–215)

1   Choose three similar half-barrels with different diameters. Paint the metal hoops that encircle the half-barrels with dark gray metal primer and then paint the half-barrels and the metal hoops with dark green paint. The paint should remain weatherproof for a fairly long time, but the half-barrels may need repainting from time to time if the paint blisters or cracks.

2   If there are no drainage holes in the base of the half-barrels, drill three 1 in (25 mm) holes in each barrel using a power drill with a spade bit.

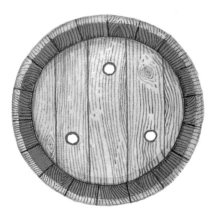

3   Follow the appropriate planting plan for each half-barrel. Remove the herbs from their pots and plant them, adding moistened potting soil to bring the plants about 1 in (25 mm) below the edge of the barrel.

small barrel

Golden thyme
(*Thymus vulgaris aurea*)
x 2, in 130 mm (5 in) pots

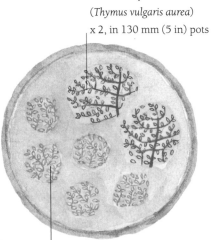

Stonecrop
(*Sedum acre*) x 5, in 80 mm (3 in) pots

medium barrel

French parsley
(*Petroselinum crispum*
'Italian') x 1, in an
80 mm (3 in) pot

Purple sage
(*Salvia officinalis*
Purpurascens Group)
x 1, in a 130 mm
(5 in) pot

White thyme
(*Thymus vulgaris albus*)
x 1, in a 130 mm (5 in) pot

Bronze fennel
(*Foeniculum vulgare* 'Purpureum')
x 3, in 80 mm (3 in) pots

Purple sage
(*Salvia officinalis*
Purpurascens Group)
x 1, in a 130 mm (5 in) pot

Lemon thyme
(*Thymus* x *citriodorus*
'Archer's Gold') x 1,
in a 130 mm (5 in) pot

French parsley
(*Petroselinum crispum*
'Italian') x 1, in an
80 mm (3 in) pot

large barrel

Gingermint
(*Mentha* x *gracilis*) x 1,
in a 130 mm (5 in) pot

Chervil
(*Anthriscus cerefolium*)
x 1, in an 80 mm (3 in) pot

Basil
(*Ocimum basilicum*) x 2,
in 80 mm (3 in) pots

Purple basil
(*Ocimum basilicum purpurascens*)
x 2, in 80 mm (3 in) pots

Rosemary (*Rosmarinus officinalis*)
x 1, in a 130 mm (5 in) pot

Summer savory (*Satureja hortensis*)
x 3, in 80 mm (3 in) pots

Parsley
(*Petroselinum crispum* 'Moss Curled')
x 1, in a 130 mm (5 in) pot

Chives
(*Allium schoenoprasum*)
x 1, in a 130 mm (5 in) pot

Tangerine sage (*Salvia elegans*)
x 1, in a 130 mm (5 in) pot

4 Clip back the purple sage each fall and
replace the biennial parsley once or twice a year
to keep the herbs to a manageable size. Replace
the annual basil every year when the frosts are
definitely over. Sow chervil twice a year if you want
a winter supply. Stonecrop needs to be kept dry.

alternative planting plans
Other herbs can also be planted in the half-
barrels, including marigolds (*Calendula
officinalis*) and heartsease (*Viola tricolor*), as in
the small barrel shown below, and the standard
golden bay (*Laurus nobilis* 'Aurea') in the medium
barrel. Nasturtiums or hops (*Humulus lupulus*)
trained up a bamboo tepee are an excellent way
of bringing height to a display.

215

an edible border

Most of the produce for the kitchen comes from the vegetable and herb gardens, but there is plenty that can be grown in the more ornamental parts of the garden. Some flowers can be eaten or used as a garnish for food, and many vegetables are so decorative that they more than earn their place in borders. Creating a border with culinary as well as decorative value can be very enjoyable and provides great economy of space in a small garden.

PLANTING SCHEME

60 *Atriplex hortensis* 'Rubra' (red orache)

30 *Calendula officinalis* (calendula)

6 *Cynara cardunculus* (cardoon)

20 *Helianthus annuus* (sunflower)

8 *Hemerocallis* (daylily)

1 The unexpected presence of decorative vegetables in a traditional flower border can give a freshness to a planting. The soil for such a border needs to be prepared in the same way as in any other border, and the planting and maintenance are just the same. These beds measure 20 x 6 ft (6 x 1.8 m). All the edible plants in them will enhance a salad, while the opening buds of the daylily can be chopped up and stir-fried.

planting plan

1 *Atriplex hortensis* 'Rubra' (red orache: edible young leaves) x 60

2 *Calendula officinalis* (pot marigold: edible flowers) x 30

3 *Cynara cardunculus* (cardoon: edible blanched stems) x 6

4 *Helianthus annuus* (sunflower: edible seed) x 20

5 *Hemerocallis* (daylily: edible opening buds) x 8

2 Where only parts of plants are being harvested, take from a different plant each time so that there is time for regrowth and to avoid giving an unbalanced appearance to the bed.

3 Not all garden plants are edible. Only those known to be safe should be eaten or used as food decoration.

alternative edible plants

The list of plants that are edible in whole or part is very long. Here are some of the most rewarding, both in terms of their decorative qualities and for culinary purposes. The less familiar edible parts of some popular vegetables are pointed out.

vegetables
Carrots (foliage)
Swiss chard (foliage)
Tomatoes (fruit)
Peas (flowers and fruit)
Corn (foliage)
Lettuce (bronze foliage)

flowering plants
Mentha (mint: leaves)
Viola odorata (heartsease: flowers)
Tropaeolum majus (nasturtium: flowers)
Thymus (thyme: leaves)
Borago officinalis (borage: flowers)
Rosa (roses: petals)
Rosmarinus officinalis (rosemary: flowers, leaves)

pergola planting

1 A pergola, whether a substantial wooden structure or a more refined metal frame, should be designed to complement the pathway borders in shape and plantings.

2 A pergola straddling a path (as left) allows the addition of several types of vegetables or fruit. The overall effect is that of an avenue of produce through which a shady walk can be taken. For a temporary display, green beans, climbing French beans, or squash and zucchini can be grown. For a more permanent display, grapes (right), apples, or pears can be trained over the arches, or a combination of apples and pears (above). Keep the climbers well trained and pruned to get the best from them. This ensures that sufficient light reaches the plants below.

a salad bed

All vegetables are best appreciated when fresh, and salad greens in particular
are crispest and most flavorful immediately after picking. Growing your own lets
you harvest as much or as little as you want, and allows you to combine, in a single
salad, the flavors of a wide variety of lettuces. Added to this is the great
satisfaction of growing your own vegetables.

MATERIALS & EQUIPMENT

stakes and string

seed of salad greens in variety

well-rotted organic matter

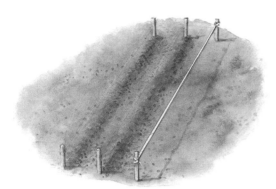

1 Prepare the soil by digging thoroughly and working in plenty of organic matter. Using stakes and string, mark out the rows, allowing for the size of the full-grown plant plus 12 in (300 mm) between each row for easy access.

2 Using the edge of a hoe, make a shallow channel, or drill, along the lines marked out. The depth depends on the seed—check the seed packet for recommendations. Scatter seed evenly along the drill, cover with soil, and pack down gently before watering. In very wet conditions, line the drill with dry sand before sowing; in dry conditions, water the drill before sowing and lightly press the seeds down into the soil.

3 Even when sown sparingly, most salad crops need thinning out. When the seedlings are big enough to handle, pull out surplus plants, leaving single plants at the required intervals (equivalent to the width of a mature plant). Any check in growth will affect size and taste—so keep the plants well-watered in dry weather to ensure that they grow continuously. The best method is to water each row individually with a watering can, making certain that the soil is thoroughly soaked.

4 Salad crops are needed year-round, but if lettuces, for example, are sown all at once then they will crop together and be over in two weeks or so. Rather than sowing full rows, it is better to sow part of a row every two weeks. Many loose-leaf lettuce varieties resprout to give a second or even third crop when cut at the base. Such cut-and-come-again varieties are excellent in a limited space.

5 Harvesting salad crops inevitably leaves ugly gaps in the rows. To make the best use of space, these can be filled by sowing radish seed; radishes are quick to mature and are ready for the kitchen just three to four weeks after sowing.

6 Perhaps the most destructive salad crop pests are slugs. An effective way to kill them is to set a beer trap— a jar, partly filled with beer, set into the soil. Alternatively, simply remove the slugs from the plants at night, when they are most active.

planting celery
Dig plenty of manure into the soil—celery demands high levels of nitrogen. Raise young celery plants from seed in the greenhouse. In the spring, set these small plants out in a narrow trench.

7 Hoe along the rows and around each plant to remove weeds. Leaf vegetables cannot be stored; cooked puréed tomatoes can be frozen; celery can be left in the ground until needed.

blanching celery
When the celery reaches a height of about 12 in (300 mm), wrap corrugated cardboard around the stems, leaving the leaves free. Fill the trench with earth, drawing it up around the cardboard "sleeve."

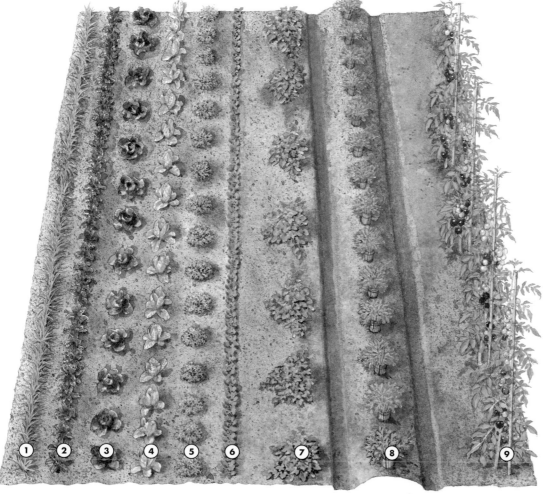

planting plan
1 Spring onions
2 Beets
3 Radicchio
4 Cos lettuce
5 Loose-leaf lettuce
6 Radishes
7 Cucumbers
8 Celery
9 Tomatoes

a strawberry bed

Although strawberries are available from stores all year round, nothing tastes quite like those eaten straight from the plant. Strawberry plants are relatively inexpensive, easy to grow, and look attractive whether in a bed or grown together in a container. With careful selection of varieties, they can be harvested from late spring right through to the fall.

MATERIALS & EQUIPMENT

stakes and string

straw for mulching

posts

flower pots

netting

7 boxwood (*Buxus sempervirens* 'Suffruticosa') per 3 ft (1 m) of hedging

5 strawberry plants per 6 ft (2 m) of strawberry row

well-rotted organic matter

1 Mark out a plot using stakes and string, checking that the corners are right angles. An area of about 15 x 10 ft (4.5 x 3 m) will provide a generous crop.

2 Strawberry beds look attractive surrounded by low hedges or raised boards. Plant young boxwood, preferably a dwarf variety such as *Buxus sempervirens* 'Suffruticosa', in the spring at 6 in (150 mm) intervals around the bed. Pinch out the tips so that the plants bush out, which may take several years. Keep the boxwood clipped to the height and width required.

3 Prepare the ground thoroughly by removing all weeds and digging in plenty of well-rotted organic matter. In late summer, buy plants that are guaranteed free from disease. Plant these at 16 in (400 mm) intervals in rows that are 2 ft (600 mm) apart. Water thoroughly; keep watered until they are established.

4 In late spring, just as the fruit is beginning to swell, mulch underneath the plants with straw, tucking it up under their leaves and stems. This helps keep the fruit off the ground. Alternatively, black plastic can be put under each plant.

wood edging
A wooden border to the strawberry bed not only looks good but is easier to prepare than a boxwood hedge border. The bed can be built up by adding plenty of well-rotted organic matter and good-quality topsoil. The board edges also help prevent straw in the bed from being blown or scattered.

pole fence surround
An alternative to a board surround is to use hazel or chestnut poles. These should be 1 in (25 mm) in diameter and split in half lengthways, then nailed to uprights that have been driven into the ground, or woven between them. Low woven hurdles can also be bought as ready-made panels.

5　Ripening fruits are a target for birds in late spring. To protect your strawberries, place short posts in the ground and drape netting over upturned flower pots—these allow the net to be moved without damaging the mesh. Weight the netting at the base.

6　Pick the strawberries by pinching through the stalk to avoid bruising the fruit. When growing strawberries, two beds should ideally be prepared because the plants begin to deteriorate if grown for more than three years in the same place. Use the beds alternately for strawberries.

a taste of Asia

Traditionally, vegetable gardeners are conservative people, adopting new plants rather slowly. For example, it was several centuries after their introduction before potatoes and tomatoes were widely grown in Europe. But in recent times gardeners have become more adventurous, matching the exciting developments in the kitchen and restaurant by growing more and more unfamiliar vegetables.

MATERIALS & EQUIPMENT

bricks • concrete • gravel

1½ x 3½ in [2 x 4] (50 x 100 mm) lumber for frame

1 x 1 in (25 x 25 mm) wood for cross members

1½ x 1½ in [2 x 2] (40 x 40 mm) lumber for frames of glass windows

galvanized screws

glass cut to size • escutcheon pins and putty

exterior-grade wood preservative or paint

saw and rabbet plane • stakes and string

well-rotted organic matter

seed and plants in variety (see page 231)

Please note: This project is more complex than others in the book.
If you are not familiar with estimating concrete or masonry techniques,
consult a professional, using this plan as a guide.

1   Many Asian vegetables can be grown successfully under cover in a temperate climate. A cold frame built on a brick base provides a warm and permanent environment. To build the brick base, first use stakes and string to mark out a rectangular trench 60 x 82 in (1.5 x 2.1 m) on its outer side, and 10 in (250 mm) wide. Dig down to a depth of 16 in (400 mm) and remove the soil.

2   Ram down 5 in (130 mm) of gravel in the base of the trench; pour and level 4 in (100 mm) of concrete on top. Lay two courses of bricks below ground level.

3   Build the rear wall so that the top is 24 in (600 mm) above ground level. The front wall should be 17 in (430 mm) above ground level. The side walls should slope between the two. The "steps" in the top of the side walls can be filled with concrete to create a smooth slope.

4   The top frame should be made from 2 x 4 (50 x 100 mm) timber, cut to fit exactly the dimensions of the brick enclosure. Join the vertical and horizontal members with a half-lap joint: saw out a section from each, half as deep as the timber itself, and as wide as the other piece.

5   Use two screws to join the shorter vertical timbers to the longer horizontals. Arrange the screws on the diagonal—if they are in line, they are likely to split the wood.

6   Treat the frame with preservative, or paint it with primer and paint. The frame can then be screwed onto the top of the brick enclosure.

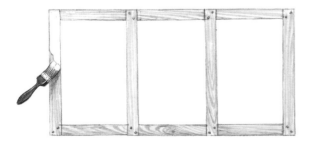

7   Nail wooden runners 1 x 1 in (25 x 25 mm) to the shorter cross members. These will prevent the lights (the glazed panels of the cold frame) from sliding sideways when fitted later.

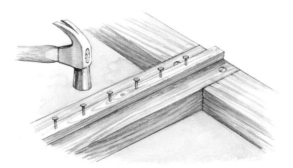

8 The simplest lights are rectangular wooden frames that hold a single sheet of glass. The three frames are made from 2 x 2 (40 x 40 mm) wood, joined at the corners with half-lap joints, made as described in step 4. The frames should be just wide enough to fit snugly between the vertical battens of the frame —take your measurements carefully from the frame itself.

9 Using a rabbet plane, cut narrow ledges, or rabbets, into the edges of the frame to hold the glass. Fit a sheet of horticultural-grade glass that has been cut to the correct size by a glazier. Secure using escutcheon pins and putty.

10 Dig the soil at the base of the enclosure, mixing in well-rotted organic matter. If this soil is not particularly deep, good garden soil or potting soil can be added on top. Sow seed lengthways across the frame in shallow drills. Stagger the sowings so that crops mature at different times. Thin as necessary.

11 Leave the windows open as much as possible, but put them on to protect the crops during cold weather. The plants will need regular watering, especially around the edges where rain may not reach.

planting plan

1 Garland chrysanthemum 'Large Leaf'
2 Mustard greens 'Southern Giant'
3 Mustard greens 'Red Giant'
4 Pak choi 'Choki'
5 Japanese celery
6 Texsel greens
7 Garland chrysanthemum 'Small Leaf'
8 Mustard greens 'Green in the Snow'
9 Choy sum 'Purple Flowering'

herbs in a mixed bed

Herb gardens need a surprising amount of upkeep, and there are times—especially from late summer onward—when they look a bit tired. One solution is to grow the herbs among other flowers in a mixed bed. When in season, the herbs add fragrance and charm to the border; other plants take over when the herbs are not at their best. Another benefit of a mixed planting is that herbs can be harvested without leaving gaps in the garden.

MATERIALS & EQUIPMENT

stakes and string

pressure-treated lumber ¾ x 3½ in [1 x 4] (20 x 100 mm) for edging

stakes ¾ x 6 in (20 x 150 mm)

stepping stones or broken slabs

gravel

sand

8 x 1 ft (2.4 m x 300 mm) heavy-duty plastic sheet

herbs and decorative plants

well-rotted organic matter

metal soil tamper

1   Draw an outline of your desired bed, planning in access to all parts of the plot from a central gravel path and stepping stones. The stepping stones can be square, circular, or irregular paving slabs; if they are not cemented in place, they can be moved if the planting is changed. The plot shown here measures 8 x 8 ft (2.4 x 2.4 m).

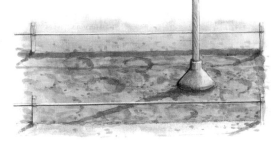

2   Use stakes and string to mark out the position of the path on the ground. Tamp down the soil firmly, so that the gravel will be almost flush with the ground when laid. Also tamp down the soil where the stepping stones are to be laid.

3   To prevent the gravel from spilling into the bed, construct a simple edging strip from lengths of ¾ x 3½ in (20 x 100 mm) lumber. For every 3 ft (900 mm) of edging board, nail in a 6 in (150 mm) upright that has been sharpened to a point.

4   Gently hammer the stakes (and edging board) into the ground along the line of the path. Line the floor of the path with heavy-duty plastic before pouring in the gravel—this will help suppress weed growth. Fill the prepared path with a 4 in (100 mm) depth of gravel and rake the surface.

5   When laying the stepping stones, set them onto a 2 in (50 mm) layer of sand to make them level.

6   Till the bed thoroughly in fall, removing any perennial weeds and adding well-rotted organic matter. In spring, till again and remove any new weeds. Place the plants, still in their pots, in place. Stand back and try to imagine them in full growth, making any necessary adjustments to their positions. Mix the plants so that the herbs are scattered throughout the bed. This not only masks them during their less interesting phases but also means that you can savor their individual fragrances more easily. Plant out, starting from the back of the plot. Water well. Rake over the border to even the soil and remove footprints. If you intend to mulch, do so now.

7 The mint and the white willowherb are both runners and are best confined to prevent their spreading over the other plants. Small areas can be controlled by planting in a bottomless bucket. Larger confined areas can be created by digging a trench around the planting and inserting a vertical layer of thick plastic, at least 12 in (300 mm) deep.

8 Draw up a complete planting plan. It is important not to underestimate the size to which some plants will grow. The plan is not sacrosanct and plants can change from year to year.

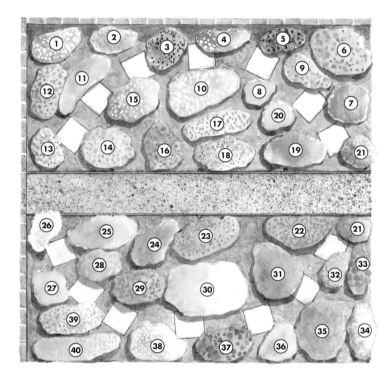

planting plan

1 *Philadelphus* 'Sybille' x 1
2 *Foeniculum vulgare* (fennel) x 3
3 *Lathyrus odoratus* (sweet pea) x 8
4 *Angelica archangelica* (angelica) x 1
5 *Oenothera biennis* (evening primrose) x 3
6 *Cynara cardunculus* (cardoon) x 1
7 *Satureja montana* (winter savory) x 1
8 *Petroselinum crispum* (parsley) x 5
9 *Borago officinalis* (borage) x 3
10 *Epilobium angustifolium* 'Album' (willowherb) x 3
11 *Mentha spicata* (mint) x 3
12 *Aster* x *frikartii* x 1
13 *Lavandula stoechas pendunculata* x 1
14 *Nepeta* x *faassennii* (catmint) x 2
15 *Allium tuberosum* (garlic chives) x 5
16 *Achillea millefolium* 'Cerise Queen' (yarrow) x 1
17 *Nepeta govaniana* x 3
18 *Lavandula angustifolia* (lavender) x 1
19 *Astrantia major* x 3
20 *Melissa officinalis* (lemon balm) x 1
21 *Laurus nobilis* (bay) x 2
22 *Thymus serpyllum* (thyme) x 3
23 *Nepeta sibirica* x 3
24 *Artemisia dracunculus* (French tarragon) x 3
25 *Origanum vulgare* (oregano) x 3
26 *Tanecetum parthenium* 'Aureum' x 2
27 *Ruta graveolens* (rue) x 1
28 *Calaminta grandiflora* (calamint) x 1
29 *Iris foetidissima* x 1
30 *Salvia officinalis* 'Icterina' (sage) x 1
31 *Levisticum officinale* (lovage) x 1
32 *Anemone* x *hybrida* x 3
33 *Allium schoenoprasum* (chives) x 5
34 *Myrrhis odorata* (sweet Cicely) x 1
35 *Rosmarinus officinalis* (rosemary) x 1
36 *Pelargonium graveolens* (scented geranium) x 3
37 *Geranium phaeum* x 1
38 *Dianthus* 'Miss Sinkins' x 3
39 *Alchemilla mollis* (lady's mantle) x 3
40 *Althaea officinalis* (marsh mallow) x 1

9 Herb gardens tend to become messy if not given regular attention. Deadhead flowering stems unless seed is required, and remove all vegetation that is dying back or already dead.

a potager

A potager, or kitchen garden, is not only productive but is also designed to look attractive. There are many ways to do this, but basically it is a question of combining the colors, shapes, and textures of plants in a well-considered layout. Paths, beds, and ornamental structures can all play valuable roles. Such a garden may be a single bed or a combination of several.

MATERIALS & EQUIPMENT

terra-cotta pots

gravel

edging bricks

pegs and string

bottle and light-colored sand

metal soil tamper

vegetable seed and plants in variety

well-rotted organic matter

1 Draw up a plan of your desired potager. In the first instance it should include only the bare bones and permanent features of the vegetable garden, including paths, edging, and any hedges and trees.

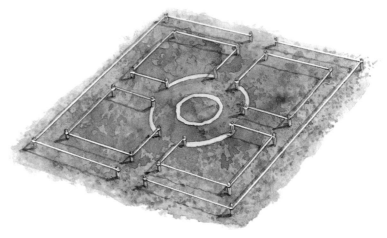

2 Thoroughly prepare the plot by removing all weeds and moving existing plants that are in the wrong place. Transfer your drawn plans to the ground using pegs and string. Curved lines may be laid out using lengths of flexible hose. Double-check all measurements.

3 It is not essential to fix the paths permanently in concrete; indeed, you may wish to enlarge or redesign the potager after a few years. Simply pack down the soil in the path areas with a metal soil tamper and add several layers of gravel. Alternatively, lay paving slabs on a bed of sand. If using gravel, put the brick edging in place before laying the path.

4 Dig the bed areas, adding as much organic matter as possible. Draw out the planting plan on each bed using a bottle of sand as an oversized pencil. Sow the seed or set out the plants according to your needs. Planting a boxwood hedge around the potager will give it a distinct boundary. Set out the young boxwood plants at 6 in (150 mm) intervals (see page 226).

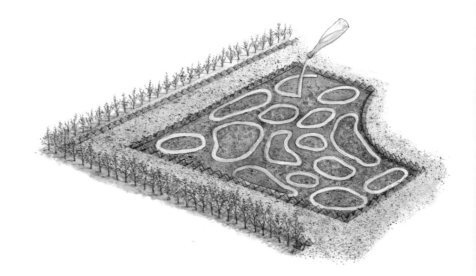

planting plan
1 Sweet peas
2 Lavender
3 Alpine strawberries
4 Mizuma greens
5 Tarragon
6 Hyssop
7 French sorrel
   (in pots)
8 Salad greens
9 Rhubarb
10 Florence fennel
11 Standard rose
12 Cardoons
13 Apple mint
14 Sage
15 Rosemary
16 Curly-leaved
   parsley
17 Squashes
18 Flat-leaved parsley
19 Ruby chard
20 Red atriplex
21 Bush tomatoes
22 Climbing rose
   ('Félicité Perpétue')
23 Chives
24 Leeks

5 Try to keep the potager looking its best throughout the summer. Harvesting plants leaves gaps that can upset the design, so keep a few young plants growing in pots and trays to plant out as replacements. Quick-germinating, fast-growing crops, such as radishes, which can be sown in situ, can also be used as fillers.

filling gaps in the design
Terra-cotta pots can be planted up and placed either as a permanent part of the display or to fill a gap temporarily. Keep several pots in reserve to use whenever there is a blank space or to replace a pot that has finished.

239

a bean arbor

A seat beneath a flower-laden arbor is a feature associated with formal ornamental gardens, but there is no reason why such a decorative refuge cannot be incorporated into a vegetable garden. Covered with runner beans, the arbor can be both beautiful and productive. It is possible to create a permanent structure or something more temporary, which can be moved from one year to the next.

MATERIALS & EQUIPMENT

ready-made arbor

stakes and string

pressure-treated lumber ¾ x 9¼ [1 x 10] (20 x 230 mm)

coarse gravel

sand

pea gravel

garden roller or metal soil tamper

cement

4 scarlet runner bean plants (*Phaseolus coccineus*) per 3 ft (1 m)

well-rotted organic matter

1   Choose an arbor frame from a garden center or mail-order supplier, or find a blacksmith who will produce a more unusual design to your specifications. Think carefully about size—you may wish to fit a table as well as a bench under the arbor—and you should allow about 12 in (300 mm) for growth of the runner beans within the frame.

2   Clear the area of ground on which you want to place the arbor. Use stakes to mark the position of the legs. Use more stakes and string to mark the edges of a seating area and approaching path, both of which will be filled with gravel.

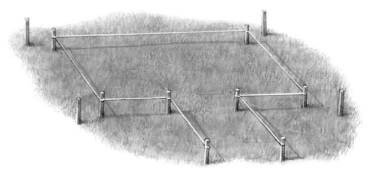

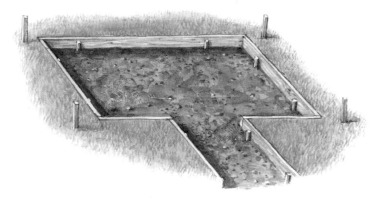

3   In the seating and path area, dig down to 8 in (200 mm) and remove the soil. Place treated boards around the dug area, securing with wooden pegs at 3 ft (1 m) intervals. Use a heavy roller or metal soil tamper to flatten the base.

4   Cover the base of the excavated area with gravel to a depth of 4 in (100 mm). Lay a middle layer of coarse gravel and sand 2 in (50 mm) deep, and cover this with 1 in (25 mm) of pea gravel. Rake the surface to level off.

5   In sheltered sites, you don't need to cement in the uprights of the arbor frame. Dig a hole for each post at least 18 in (450 mm) deep. Add a 4 in (100 mm) layer of gravel and place the framework in position. Refill the holes, ramming down the earth firmly with a tamper. In exposed sites, it is best to cement the framework into position because wind pressure on the plant-covered arbor can be significant.

6   After the threat of frost has passed, dig the soil around the arbor and plant the runner beans. Plant a seedling against each post and then at 10 in (250 mm) intervals. Scatter slug pellets around the base. Water thoroughly.

7   Beans will naturally twine up and over the arbor, but it may be necessary to direct them at the initial stages to ensure that there is even coverage. There is no need to tie the stems—it is enough just to tuck them in.

8   Don't let the beans dry out, especially once the flowers have started to form. To encourage bushier growth, pinch out the tops of the stems when they reach the middle of the arbor. The beans produce a display of red, pink, or white flowers, depending on variety.

9   Pick the beans when about 6 in (150 mm) long. Harvest every three to four days, taking the beans before their seeds swell. Don't leave old pods on the plants; they inhibit the formation of new ones.

tools and techniques

EQUIPMENT

For the gardener
Many of the projects in this book can be undertaken with
the bare essentials of gardening equipment.

Use a wheelbarrow for fetching and moving pots and
mixing soil, and a hand truck or dolly for transporting
larger containers. A heavy-duty drop cloth or a specially
made cloth with handles makes cleanup easier.

Indispensable hand tools include an old kitchen knife
for weeding pots, a hand fork and trowel, a dibble to make
holes for seeds or young plants, pruners, sharp scissors,
shears, and a pruning saw.

Old garden tools are often much nicer than new ones;
buy them cheaply from secondhand stores. Failing that,
invest in some stainless-steel tools, which wear well and
are easy to clean.

For watering, you need a watering can and a garden
hose. Use a hose-end sprayer to apply liquid fertilizers and
pesticides. Gardening can be a grubby business and harsh
on the hands; wear gardening gloves for protection.

For the woodworker
There are few complicated procedures in the construction
projects described in this book. If you can put a piece of
wood and screw separate pieces together, you will be able
to manage most of them—but seek professional advice if
you are in any doubt. When buying and cutting wood, use
English measurements. Metric sizes are also provided.

**Please note that in some cases the conversions are not
direct.** If your lumberyard uses English measurements,
stick with inches and feet.

Use a hand saw (crosscut) or a circular saw for cutting
lumber and plywood to size. A workbench or a sturdy pair
of sawhorses is useful when cutting. A sabersaw is
especially handy when making curved cuts, but a coping
saw will also do the job.

The most versatile type of hammer is the claw hammer,
which has one end for driving nails and a curved claw for
removing them.

For drilling holes, use a power drill or a brace and bit.
Most structures are secured with screws. A screwdriver
with a Phillips head is recommended.

Also useful are a pair of C-clamps (for keeping work
steady or holding pieces together) and a block plane.

For painting
Ordinary household paintbrushes are all that is required
for most of the projects, but for decorative details, an
artist's brush will give more accuracy.

Before you begin to paint, make sure the surface is
smooth and clean; a soft-bristled dusting brush works best.
Use mineral spirits to clean oil-based paint from brushes.

Other items of general equipment that may be useful
include old rags and protective plastic or paper drop
cloths. Exterior-grade wood filler can be used to fill cracks
and indents.

For metal projects

The metal constructions described in this book are relatively simple and need only a few special items of equipment, such as a pair of tin cutters for cutting lead or sheet-metal facings and trimmings.

A hacksaw is the best tool for cutting thicker metals. When shaping metal, use a vise on a bench together with a mallet to help bend the strips and form corners.

For gilding, a range of metal leaf (in gold, silver, aluminum, and other metals) is available. When handling lead, wear a pair of protective gloves.

WOODWORKING TECHNIQUES

Glues and fasteners

The adhesive recommended for use in these projects is waterproof carpenter's glue. Before gluing, always make sure the surfaces are free of dust and grease. Let the adhesive dry overnight to achieve its full strength.

Phillips screws are easiest to work with, especially when using an electric screwdriver. Choose screws that are plated to protect them from rust.

When screwing two pieces of wood together, start with a bit that is slightly smaller than the screw. Drill a pilot hole from the first piece and into the second. Next, using a bit that matches the thickness of the screw, drill through the first piece only. Then attach the two pieces with the screw. If you are drilling into sound wood and are more than 2 in (50 mm) from an edge, it is usually safe to skip the pilot hole.

When using nails, choose galvanized ones to prevent rust. For a neat finish, use a nail set to punch your nail below the surface of the wood and fill the indentation with wood putty.

Lumber

Lumber is broadly classified into two categories: softwood and hardwood. Softwood, which comes from a variety of coniferous trees, is usually suitable for the projects in this book because it is inexpensive and easy to work with. Before applying any other finish, treat it with exterior-grade wood preservative.

Lumber is available with two types of surfaces: rough-sawn and surfaced (smooth). When buying lumber, be sure to specify what you want. Rough-sawn wood is good for certain treatments, especially if you plan to use a decorative stain or want a rustic look. Surfaced lumber is better for wood that will be painted, especially if you plan to use high-gloss paint.

Softwood

Softwood comes in several different grades. For most projects, you will want "select," which is free of defects and knots. Lumber is sold by what's called "nominal size," which is the size of the wood (thickness x width) before it is milled. For instance, what's commonly referred to as a 2 x 4 is actually $1\frac{1}{2}$ x $3\frac{1}{2}$ in. (Length is not diminished by processing.) The projects in this book feature the nominal size in brackets [] when applicable. Sizes indicated on lumber are actual dimensions—not nominal sizes.

Plywood

Exterior-grade plywood is available in several thicknesses: $\frac{3}{8}$, $\frac{1}{2}$, $\frac{5}{8}$, and $\frac{3}{4}$ in.

Hardwood

Oak and teak are the best hardwoods for outdoor use, but they are expensive and hard to work with. Use a stained finish with oak and teak; it is difficult to keep paint on these woods for the long term.

Preservatives

Unpreserved wood should be treated with exterior-grade wood preservative, which prevents rot, insect damage, and disease. The preservatives are toxic to plants, so they must be applied well in advance of planting.

Stains

Most effective on rough-sawn lumber, stains look best in muted colors. Choose a nonchalking, or sealer, type.

Paints

A wide range of paint types is available for exterior use on wood, including exterior-grade latex and oil-based paint. For concrete and masonry you can use most types of paint, but there are also special formulations for concrete and masonry. For metal, use specially formulated high-gloss metal paint.

MAKING A BASIC WINDOW BOX

The instructions below explain how to make the basic structures for an herbal window box (pages 26–29), a raised scented window box (pages 34–37), a lead-faced trough (pages 52–55), and the balcony herb boxes (pages 38–41). Before starting one of these projects, refer to the appropriate list below to establish the quantities and types of wood that you will need. See the individual project for more instructions and planting advice.

Materials & equipment
• screwdriver
• power drill with a 1 in (25 mm) spade bit or a brace and bit
• wood screws 1½ in (40 mm) long

For an herbal window box
• 4 rough-sawn side boards ¾ x 5½ x 10 in [1 x 6]
  (20 x 150 x 250 mm)
• 4 front and back boards ¾ x 5½ x 31 in [1 x 6]
  (20 x 150 x 780 mm)
• 4 uprights 1½ x 1½ x 10 in [2 x 2](40 x 40 x 250 mm)
• 2 battens 1½ x 1½ x 26 in [2 x 2] (40 x 40 x 660 mm)
• 2 battens 1½ x 1½ x 7 in [2 x 2] (40 x 40 x 180 mm)
• 1 piece of exterior-grade plywood
  ½ x 9¾ x 28¾ in (10 x 245 x 750 mm)

For a raised scented window box and a lead-faced trough
• 2 exterior-grade plywood side boards
  ¾ x 6½ x 8 in (20 x 160 x 200 mm)
• 2 exterior-grade plywood front and back boards
  ¾ x 8 x 36 in (20 x 200 x 900 mm)
• 2 uprights 1½ x 1½ x 8 in [2 x 2] (40 x 40 x 150 mm)
• 2 battens 1½ x 1½ x 31½ in [2 x 2] (40 x 40 x 810 mm)
• 2 battens 1½ x 1½ x 3½ in [2 x 2] (40 x 40 x 90 mm)
• 1 piece of exterior-grade plywood
  ¾ x 6¼ x 34¼ in (20 x 155 x 855 mm)

For each balcony herb box
• 4 surfaced softwood side boards
  ¾ x 3½ x 8 in [1 x 4] (20 x 90 x 200 mm)
• 4 surfaced softwood front and back boards
  ¾ x 3½ x 36 in [1 x 4] (20 x 90 x 900 mm)
• 4 uprights 1½ x 1½ x 7 in [2 x 2] (40 x 40 x 180 mm)
• 2 battens 1½ x 1½ x 31½ in [2 x 2] (40 x 40 x 810 mm)
• 2 battens 1½ x 1½ x 5 in [2 x 2] (40 x 40 x 130 mm)
1 piece of exterior-grade plywood
  ¾ x 7¾ x 34¼ in (20 x 200 x 850 mm)

1   Drill pilot holes in each corner of the side boards and screw the side boards to two of the uprights. Attach the remaining side boards to the other two uprights. Note that the raised scented window box is composed of single pieces of plywood.

2   Drill pilot holes in the front and back boards and screw them to the two side boards as shown, ensuring that the bottom boards are flush with the base of the uprights. Turning the box on its side makes this step easier.

3   Screw the two long battens to the lower boards of the front and back panels from the inside so that they are flush with the base of the box. In the same way, screw the short battens to the lower boards of the side panels.

4   Using a power drill with a 1 in (25 mm) spade bit, drill eight evenly spaced holes in the plywood. Cut a square notch from each corner of the plywood so it fits around the uprights, and slide into position on top of the battens.

CUTTING MITERED CORNERS

The most efficient way to cut a mitered joint in a piece of wood is to use a miter box. This simple device has slots to guide the saw. The best type of saw to use for wood that is less than 2 in (50 mm) thick is a tenon saw. Hold the piece of wood against the side of the box and make angled cuts (usually 45°). Square ends can also be cut using the miter box, as shown above.

MAKING A TRELLIS FENCE PANEL AND CORNER UNIT

Each corner unit of the trellis-enclosed herb garden shown on pages 116–19 consists of two trellis fence panels mounted onto three corner posts. If it's available, use rough-sawn, pressure-treated lumber, or coat the lumber in exterior-grade wood preservative.

Materials & equipment
For each panel
- 511 in (13 m) lattice* 1 x 2 in (25 x 50 mm)
- galvanized finishing nails 1 in (25 mm) long

For each corner unit
- 3 pressure-treated posts, 3½ x 3½ x 36 [4 x 4] (90 x 90 x 900 mm)
- 3 post anchors
- 2 pieces lumber ¾ x 2½ x 74 in [1 x 3] (20 x 80 x 1830 mm)
- timber block for hammering post anchors
- sledgehammer
- galvanized screws 3 in (80 mm) long
- galvanized finishing nails 2 in (50 mm) long

1 From the 1 x 2 in (25 x 50 mm) lattice, cut two 74 in (1830 mm) pieces and two 24 in (600 mm) uprights. On the longer pieces mark five equal sections with a pencil. Nail them to the uprights with 1 in (25 mm) nails.

2 From the 1 x 2 in (25 x 50 mm) lattice, cut five 31½ in (790 mm) pieces and nail them to the frame at the points marked with a pencil. Cut off the pieces from the diagonals where they overlap the frame, as shown above.

3 From the 1 x 2 in (25 x 50 mm) lattice, cut five 31½ in (790 mm) pieces and nail them to the frame in the same way. Cut off the excess wood. Make the second panel.

4 Place the timber block over each of the metal post anchors and hammer them into the ground so the anchor top protrudes only slightly above the soil. Space the anchors at intervals of 74 in (1830 mm).

5 Knock each corner post into a post anchor, as shown.

6 Drill four holes in each of the panel uprights and screw the uprights into the three posts using the galvanized screws.

7 To finish off, nail a 74 in (1830 mm) piece of ¾ x 2½ in (20 x 80 mm) capping to the top of each trellis panel.

*A note about 1 x 2 lattice: Large lumberyards often stock clear pine lattice. If you cannot get this size, ask to have it cut from larger boards.

SOLID BOUNDARIES

Many people regard brick and stone walls as the ultimate in boundaries. Although the materials are expensive, walls are long-lasting and provide an ideal home for many climbing and tender plants. Walls should be well made, so if you have any doubts about your ability to build a secure, safe structure, hire a professional. However, two or three courses (rows) of bricks or walls up to 18 in (450 mm) high should be within the ability of most gardeners.

For most purposes, walls should be at least two bricks wide—that is, about 9 in (230 mm)—although a single skin of bricks can be used for walls of only two or three courses. The pattern that brick makes is important in regard to the strength of the wall in addition to its appearance.

Mixing concrete

You can buy concrete as a ready-to-use mix (just add water), or mix it yourself. The ready-to-use concrete is easier, especially if you need less than 1 cubic yard (1 m³). An 80 lb bag of mix makes about ⅔ cubic foot. You can mix one bag at a time in a garden wheelbarrow; two sacks at a time in a contractor's wheelbarrow.

If you want to make your own, the ratios are as follows: 1 part portland cement, 2.5 parts sand, 2.5 parts gravel and 0.5 parts water. The amount of water can vary quite a bit. Add only a little at a time. The easiest way to mix concrete is to use a mixing drum or a rented concrete mixer. Add water a little at a time until the mixture is of the right consistency. Avoid making it too wet (see step 3, right). If you do not have access to a mixer, follow the instructions below.

2   A little at a time, pour water into the crater. It should not run out of the crater.

3   Mix the concrete and the water and add more water if necessary. Slice the mix with a spade. The edges should hold straight. If the edges crumble, add more water. If the edges fall over, add more ingredients.

Brick bonds

The common bonds, or patterns, used in bricklaying are English bond and Flemish bond (both two bricks thick) and running bond (a single-brick thickness). Bricks laid long-edge out are called stretchers. Bricks laid short-edge out are called headers.

1   Place the concrete mix or dry ingredients on a large board (or in a wheelbarrow). Mound it in the center of the board, and create a crater in the center of the mound.

English bond
Two bricks deep, this pattern comprises one, three, or five courses of stretchers to one course of headers.

Flemish bond
Two bricks deep, this bond has one, three, or five stretchers to one header per course.

Running bond
A single brick deep, this bond comprises only stretchers. These must be laid in a staggered formation to achieve maximum strength.

Checking level top and side
It is essential that walls are level in all directions, and a level should be used repeatedly as a wall is built. Build the ends (and corners) first and, using a line as a guide, build the center one row at a time.

RAISED BEDS

Raised beds can be a great asset in a small garden. They are particularly effective in small town gardens where they have been designed to complement the house. Such low structures are ideal for a novice builder.

Raised beds of brick, stone, or concrete blocks require foundations. To provide drainage, leave gaps in the vertical pointing in the lower courses of the brickwork. To prepare the bed, put a layer of broken rocks in the base and fill with good soil and well-rotted organic matter.

Foundations
Create foundations of gravel and concrete, then build the raised bed, one course at a time. Larger beds need a bond two bricks deep.

Drainage
Drainage is provided by means of broken stones in the base and sand added to the soil and well-rotted organic material.

Other materials
Railroad ties do not need foundations. Lay them on a flat base and stagger the corner joints, leaving small gaps for drainage.

SOIL PREPARATION

The most important aspect of creating a border is thorough preparation. Without it, even the best designs are likely to fail after a year or two, smothered by weeds or starved of nutrients and moisture.

Remove all perennial weeds before planting begins. Even a small piece of root will re-emerge as a weed, by which time it might be difficult to remove it without digging out the whole border again. In lighter soils it may be possible to dig the soil and remove any weeds at the same time, while on heavier soils it may be necessary to use a weedkiller; if so, always follow the directions on the package. Dig the soil in the fall and plant in the spring. This will allow any small piece of weed left in the soil to reveal itself so that it can be removed. In areas with warmer winters it is also possible to dig in spring and plant in fall.

DOUBLE DIGGING

All borders should be dug over but they will be better, especially on heavy soils, if they are double dug—as described below—so that the lower layer of earth is also broken up. Do not dig if the soil is too wet. At the same time as the border is dug, as much well-rotted organic

1 Dig a trench 12–18 in (300–450 mm) wide and 12 in (300 mm) deep. Reserve the removed earth.

2 Work the trench for a further 12 in (300 mm) and add organic matter. Dig out the next trench and use the earth to fill the first.

3 As before, work through the layer below, breaking up the ground with a fork and adding organic material.

4 When you reach the end of the border, fill the final trench with the reserved earth.

SOIL CONDITIONERS

Chipped or composted bark Best used as a mulch
Commercially prepared conditioners Good but expensive
Farmyard manure Good all-round conditioner as long as it does not contain weed seed
Garden compost Good all-round conditioner as long as it does not contain weed seed
Leaf mulch Excellent conditioner and mulch
Peat Little nutrient value and breaks down too quickly to be of great value
Seaweed Excellent conditioner, includes plenty of minerals
Spent hops Good conditioner but limited nutrients
Spent mushroom compost Good conditioner and mulch; includes lime

matter as possible should be incorporated into the soil. This not only improves the structure of the soil but provides nutrients for the plants. Its fibrous nature also helps to preserve moisture deep in the soil where the plants' roots need it. Once the soil has been dug over, leave it for several months. This will allow the rain and frost to break it down and kill any pests. Residual weeds will also reappear. Avoid walking on the area while it is weathering.

GARDEN COMPOST

One of the best ways of providing organic material for the garden is to make your own compost. Almost any plant material can be used as long as it is not too woody and does not contain weed seeds. Avoid diseased material and virulent weeds; uncooked vegetable waste is recommended.

Place all the material in a container that has air holes in the sides. Avoid creating too thick a layer of any one material, such as grass cuttings. Keep the bin moist but covered so that the compost retains heat and to prevent it becoming too wet and chilled in heavy rain. Turn the heap occasionally.

If possible, have two bins, one for collecting material; three allows a bin for rotting down.

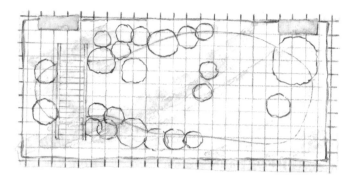

PLANNING A BORDER

Before you draw up a plan for a border, decide what you are aiming to achieve. For example, you may want a low-maintenance border, a bright, vibrant border, or a romantic display in pastel tones. Is it more important to you to create dramatic effects with foliage or to have plenty of flowers for cutting?

Consider also the position of the border and its physical attributes. Does it get plenty of sun or is it in perpetual shade? Is the soil acid or alkaline? Is it wet or dry or just about right? Is it heavy or sandy? All these factors have a bearing on how much work you will have to put in and on what plants you can and cannot grow. For example, if you live in an area where there is chalky soil, you will not be able to grow rhododendrons.

Then decide what plants you want to use to create the desired effect. This is best done over at least one season so you can visit other gardens, notebook in hand, compiling a list of desirable plants. Looking through books is also another stimulating source of ideas. After you have compiled an initial list, the next stage is to find out whether your preferred plants can be obtained locally or if tracking them down will involve a long search. Adjust your list accordingly.

You are now ready to plot the planting. Using graph paper, draw the border to scale and then mark the location of each plant, sketching them at their eventual spread (above). You do not need to be good at drawing to produce a useful plan. Adjacent colors should coordinate and the border should have an even spread of interest throughout the year. It is a good idea to draw the bed at different seasons so you can assess how successful the plan will be through the year, and from the front to compare the plants' relative heights. If problems appear as you are making the sketches, it is much easier to correct them at this stage than it would be after planting.

PLANTING

Rake or lightly fork the soil, removing any weeds. If only a small amount of organic material was added when the soil was being prepared, granular fertilizer can be raked into the surface. Follow the directions on the package.

Shrubs and trees should ideally be planted from late fall to early spring, and perennials in either fall or spring. If you live in a cold winter area, spring planting is best. Annuals should not be planted out until the threat of frost is passed if they are tender, or in fall or spring if they are hardy. Position the plants, still in their pots, in the border so that you can get an idea of how the display will look, and make any necessary adjustments.

Dig a hole wider than each plant's rootball and insert the plant so that it is at the same depth as it was in its pot or, if it is bare-rooted, in its previous bed. If the roots have become pot-bound or tangled, gently tease them out and spread them in the hole. Fill the hole and pack the soil around the roots. When planting a tree or a shrub, dig a much larger hole than the plant's rootball and dig plenty of well-rotted organic material into the bottom of the hole. Mix some into the soil that will go back into the hole once the plant is in place.

If staking the tree or shrub, position the stake before planting so that the roots will not be damaged by driving it through them.

USING A MULCH

Once all the plants are in the bed, water them thoroughly, rake over the surface to level it off and apply a mulch.

Mulches cover the surface of the soil, helping to keep moisture in and preventing weed seed from germinating; they can also create an attractive background for plants.

Organic mulches consist of bark, leaf mold, spent mushroom compost, or even grass-cuttings and straw. Inorganic mulches include plastic sheets (which should be covered with soil, gravel, or other stones), gravel, or pebbles.

SOWING SEED

Direct sowing: annuals
If clumps of plants are required, mark out the ground with fine sand before sowing.

Direct sowing: perennials
1 Dig the soil well, then rake it to produce a fine texture for sowing.

2 Make a shallow drill with the edge of a hoe, using a guide line if necessary. This can be made using stakes and a length of string.

3 Pour some water into the drill. This will help to consolidate the hollow and will ensure the seeds receive adequate moisture.

4 Sow the seed, sprinkling a fine line into the drill. Do not overfill—overcrowding can starve seedlings of nourishment.

5 Draw the soil back into the drill with the back of the rake and water gently.

Direct sowing
Direct sowing is a technique used for seed that are planted directly into the ground—often in the place in which they are to grow. If you are sowing annuals into a border, break down the soil into a fine texture with a rake. If several clumps of plants are required, mark out each area with some sand so that it is easy to see where to sow. Scatter the seeds over the required area; gently rake them in. Water with a fine-rosed watering can.

If sowing perennials in rows, make a shallow drill with the edge of a hoe, using a guide line if necessary. Pour a little water into the drill and scatter seed along it. Draw the soil back into the drill and water.

Pot sowing

If only a few plants are required, or if it is necessary to sow the seeds in gentle heat, they should be sown in a tray or pot. Fill the pot with a good seed-starting soil and tap it to settle the contents; level and lightly press it down. Sow the seed thinly and cover with a layer of fine sand or compost. Water carefully.

Sowing in a pot
Once the seeds have been sprinkled in a pot, cover with soil or fine sand, as recommended on the seed packet.

Planting in a tray
Once seedlings have grown, they should be pricked out carefully and planted in individual pots to continue growing.

Many annuals need to be placed in a warm environment such as a propagator or heated greenhouse, but perennials rarely require heat and can be kept outside in a sheltered place. Keep moist until the seeds germinate and then prick out into trays or individual pots. Tender seedlings that have been sheltered should be hardened off in a cold frame before planting out after the threat of frost has passed.

Planting bulbs

As a general guide, make sure the planting hole for a bulb is at least three times as deep as the bulb is tall.

BULBS

Spring-flowering bulbs should be planted during the fall; summer- and fall-flowering bulbs should be planted in spring. As a rule, the depth of the planting hole should be at least three times the height of the bulb.

Some plants can be relied upon to increase with little attention. These are often naturalized bulbs, those that have been left to grow in grass or under trees. If they become congested after a few years, lift and divide them.

BUYING PLANTS

Garden centers sell a reasonably extensive range of plants, but specialist nurseries have a much larger and more varied selection. Many nurseries also send plants by mail order. Place your order early because demand can outstrip supply for many catalog plants, and inform the nursery if you expect to be away when the plants are expected to arrive— otherwise you might come home to a box of dead plants.

When buying plants, there is no need always to go for the largest specimen. A medium-sized plant that is free from pests and diseases is the best option. Avoid any plant that is pot-bound (below).

The alternative to buying plants is to grow your own from seed, by division or from cuttings. This is a much cheaper approach but plants will need time to mature. Rare plants are often available only as seed.

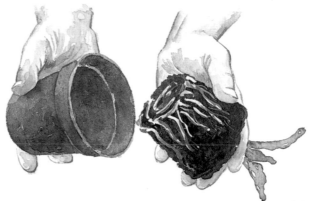

care and maintenance

CONTAINERS

When deciding what sort of containers to have in your garden, either start by choosing the plants and find containers suited to the character and habit of the plants, or start with the containers and devise planting schemes to suit them. The second option has advantages, in that most containers remain in the same place all year around and should complement the character and scale of the setting.

Consider where in the garden you need plant interest and what sort of container would look good in that spot. To be appreciated from a distance, the pot needs to be bold and simple in outline. The height of the planting must also be decided in relation to the rest of the garden; generally, the taller the planting, the larger the container that is needed.

Elaborate detail is best in a foreground location where it can be seen clearly, and the same applies to planting—complex schemes using delicate plants are best seen up close, where their detail can be fully appreciated.

The color of your material should be chosen to harmonize with the house and the rest of the garden as well as with the intended planting scheme. As a general rule, materials that weather and get a patina are more appealing; hand-thrown terra cotta quickly takes on an aged look. Lead, stone, and cast stone also age gracefully, and the process can be speeded up by applying vinegar in the case of lead, and yogurt, milk, or liquid manure in the case of stone and cast stone. One way to age a pot quickly is to place it under trees.

Cast iron and wood both need to be painted or stained to preserve them. Use a faded blue-gray green, referred to as "Versailles blue," a color often seen on the shutters of old houses in Italy and France.

CARING FOR CONTAINERS

Containers need to be scrupulously cleaned and scrubbed before planting; scrub them well on the inside with clean water, but try to preserve any weathering on the outside. Some containers are best used with plastic liners, especially if you change plants with the seasons. Plastic liners are particularly useful for large Versailles cases and urns. Check that your terra cotta is frostproof if you are going to leave it outside all year around. In winter, even hardy plants in pots will need protection from frost—wrap the pot with burlap (as shown below), straw, or bubble wrap. Where plants are in liners, pack straw between the plastic pot and container for protection. In early fall or spring examine the condition of your containers and repaint them if necessary.

All containers need good drainage. Make sure there are enough holes to let out excess moisture and put in a thin layer of pot shards or gravel in the base of pots.

PLANTING MEDIUM

Different plants require different types of soil. For semi-permanent plantings, use potting soil that has been amended with compost or well-rotted manure. For seasonal plantings, use multi-purpose potting soil. Some plants have specific requirements. For instance, special soils are available for bulbs, and very gritty free-draining soil-based composts are recommended for some alpine and rock plants. Peat-based mixtures are appropriate for containers because they are light, but they also have a tendency to dry out, so are unsuitable for plants that are difficult to water. Loam-based mixtures offer a more stable alternative but carry more weight. Also available are bark, coir, and wood-fiber composts that work well in containers.

POTTING PLANTS

The size of the container should complement the size of the planting and needs to be large enough to contain the rootball and sustain growth. Some plants dislike being repotted repeatedly and do not mind being root-bound, whereas others need to be regularly potted on as they grow. Most seasonal plantings, if properly fed and watered, can stand being in a confined pot.

For a shrub or tree, start off with a large container that will support its growth for a number of years before the inevitable repotting. Some Versailles cases are specifically designed for ease of repotting; the sides can be removed. Such a design might be suitable for large plants, such as orange and lemon trees, camellias, and greenhouse tropicals.

When planting a multiple seasonal display, it is sometimes necessary to crowd the plants to create the desired effect. This would not be appropriate for permanent plantings but in this case, as long as the roots have space to grow down, the plants will survive.

For permanent plantings, be more careful with rootball placement. Single specimens should be placed in the center of the pot and packed down. It is also best to make sure the finished soil surface is at least 1 in (25 mm) below the top edge of the container so that there is space for a water reservoir. In the case of standards, choose a specimen with an upright and secure stem (stake if necessary) because it is difficult to correct this later.

Climbing plants can have supports fixed in the soil or to the container—there is a wide range of stakes, metal shapes, and trellis obelisks available that you can construct yourself or buy ready-made.

FEEDING AND WATERING

In summer, watering is the key to successful container gardening. Small pots, particularly those made of terra cotta, dry out very quickly, and during spells of hot weather they will need watering twice a day—in the early morning and in the evening, to avoid sunburn to wet leaves. Water larger pots only once a day. Always soak the plant thoroughly by filling the reservoir at the top up to the brim. If you are using a hose, use one with a fine spray so that the water pressure does not wash away any soil.

Reduce watering as the growing season comes to an end. In winter most plants need only to be kept from drying out, so check them every few days to make sure they are still moist. In some cases plants that are dormant in winter prefer the soil to be almost dry—check individual plants for special needs. A useful way to conserve moisture is to place a layer of mulch over the soil. There are various methods for feeding container-grown plants. Slow-release granules are good for long-term plantings—sprinkle them onto the surface of the soil and work them into the top layer of the soil. Other chemical fertilizers can be mixed into the compost when planting. Liquid fertilizers are diluted in water and used as part of the watering regime. Foliar feeds are sprayed on for instant effect, and organic material can be used as a top dressing. Use homemade compost, well-rotted manure, or blood and bonemeal, applied during the growing season.

When fertilizing, always apply at the recommended rates. Also keep in mind that some plants thrive best in relatively poor soil.

PEST AND DISEASES

Plants that are stressed by poor watering and feeding are more vulnerable to attack, so the surest way to prevent the invasion of pests and diseases is to take the best possible care of your plants and containers; cleanliness of pots and tools helps to keep bacterial diseases at bay, as does keeping a regular eye on their health. Plants are subject to three groups of diseases: bacterial, fungal, and viral, the last of which is untreatable—destruction of the plant is the only remedy. Below are some typical examples of bacterial leaf spot (left) and powdery mildew (right). Benomyl is the most useful spray for bacterial leaf spot, blackspot, fungal leaf spot, and powdery mildew; spray only on calm days after sunset so as not to harm beneficial insects. The most common pests to attack container plants are aphids (greenfly and blackfly); these can be sprayed with insecticidal soap or neem-based sprays. Always identify the pest before using any treatment.

Store sprays and chemicals away from children and pets, and wear gloves and a mask as directed.

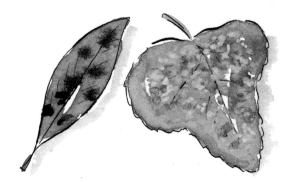

MAINTAINING BORDERS

Staking, deadheading, regular watering, and weeding all contribute to a thriving border.

Pea-stick supports
These are versatile, flexible supports that can be drawn together and tied to provide infrastructure for vulnerable plants.

Net support
A net support is a permanent device. The plant grows up and through the mesh which, in time, will be hidden by foliage.

String and stakes
Stakes with a network of strings are useful as a temporary support for larger, spreading shrubs until they are established.

Staking
Plants that could blow over or become top-heavy in rain need to be staked. Tall flower spikes, such as delphiniums, can be supported by individual canes, while clumps can be held by pea-sticks, netting supported between posts, or by specially designed supports. Stake the plants when they are half-grown; do not wait until they blow over.

Trees and shrubs should be staked with a single or double stake. For most trees it is enough to use a single tie low down, 12 in (300 mm) from the ground. For standards and spindly trees, use a taller stake and two ties.

Staking trees
A single tie should be placed low down to support a tree. This will give sufficient extra stability until the tree is established.

Staking standard bushes
Standards need a taller stake than most trees and two ties (the first tie is shown here, positioned high up the stem).

Deadheading
Unless you want to collect the seed or save the seedheads, cut off any dead or dying flowers. Many perennials, including nepeta, several perennial geraniums, lady's mantle, and oriental poppies, should be cut to the ground after flowering; this will encourage the growth of a fresh crop of leaves, and the plant will then be useful for foliage effect.

Watering
Water plants in dry conditions, making certain that they get a thorough soaking. Do not water in full sun. Feeding should not be necessary if the border is top dressed regularly. Every fall, fork in the organic mulch and replace

it with a layer of well-rotted manure or garden compost. Dig this into the beds in spring and reapply the usual mulch.

Weeding

Remove any weeds on sight. Regular checks will keep weeds under control; if left, they can become difficult and time-consuming to eradicate. By remaining vigilant, it is possible to keep weeds under control. Chemical herbicides should be avoided on a planted area.

Fall care

Most perennials need cutting back in fall. This task can be left until spring so that the old stems give some protection to the crown from frosts, but tidying during the dormant season means that there is less to do during the spring rush.

PRUNING

Ornamental trees and evergreen shrubs generally do not need pruning, except to remove any dead or dying branches, although you may want to remove stems for aesthetic reasons. By contrast, most deciduous shrubs benefit from regular attention. The aim is to keep the bush healthy and vigorous so that it produces good foliage and flowers. To do this, up to a third of the old wood should be cut out each year, encouraging new growth. Each plant has unique pruning requirements. Before you cut, learn about the plant and how it should be pruned.

Pruning and maintaining climbers

Twining plants and plants that produce tendrils, such as honeysuckle and clematis, do best with wirework support or trellis, or climbing over another plant. Clinging climbers such as ivy need no additional support. The sheer weight of an untended climber can damage a support, while overcrowding can adversely affect flower production. Pruning ensures an attractive framework and promotes vigorous growth and plentiful flowers.

Roses

Climbing and rambling roses can be very vigorous and need to be tied to a structure. They create good cover, but benefit greatly from pruning and training. Find out the specific pruning needs of your rose before you prune. Deadheading helps growth but should not be carried out if you want hips.

Pruning a climbing rose
Do not prune during the first year. After that, only prune main shoots if they grow beyond their allotted space, but prune side shoots by two-thirds.

Pruning a rambling rose
Do not prune in the first year. Then remove two or three whole stems each year (this is easier done in sections); cut back the remaining main stems by a third and side shoots by two-thirds.

Clematis

Pruning clematis can be rather complicated because different varieties of the plant need to be treated in different ways.

There are three groups of clematis, and it is essential to know to which group a specimen belongs to avoid destructive or insufficient pruning. Examples of clematis varieties and their groups are given below. Plants belonging to the first group should be pruned in fall, while plants in the other two groups should be pruned in early spring. Correct pruning will encourage full growth and maximum flowering.

Clematis group 1

Early-flowering species that flower on the previous year's shoots: Only prune out dead material. If you want to prevent the plant from becoming too large and heavy, remove a few stems each year.

Clematis group 2

Large-flowered varieties that flower early to mid-season on new shoots from the previous year's stems: Prune old wood lightly.

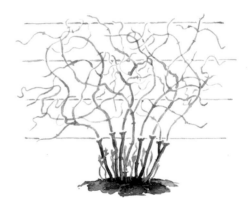

Clematis group 3

Large-flowered varieties that flower late on new wood: These can be cut right back to just above a strong pair of buds.

EXAMPLES OF CLEMATIS

C. 'Abundance' 3	C. 'Little Nell' 3
C. alpina 1	C. macropetala 1
C. armandii 1	C. 'Marie Boisselot' 2
C. 'Barbara Dibley' 2	C. 'Miss Bateman' 2
C. 'Barbara Jackman' 2	C. montana 1
C. 'Bill MacKenzie' 3	C. 'Mrs Cholmondeley' 2
C. cirrhosa 1	C. 'Nelly Moser' 2
C. 'Comtesse de Bouchaud' 3	C. 'Niobe' 2
C. 'Countess of Lovelace' 2	C. 'Perle d'Azur' 3
C. 'Daniel Deronda' 2	C. 'Rouge Cardinal' 3
C. 'Doctor Ruppel' 2	C. 'Royal Velours' 3
C. 'Duchess of Albany' 3	C. 'Star of India' 2
C. 'Elsa Späth' 2	C. tangutica 3
C. 'Ernest Markham' 2	C. 'The President' 2
C. 'Etoile Violette' 3	C. tibetana 3
C. 'Gipsy Queen' 3	C. 'Ville de Lyon' 3
C. 'Hagley Hybrid' 3	C. viticella 3
C. 'H. F. Young' 2	C. 'Vyvyan Pennell' 2
C. 'Jackmanii' 3	C. 'W. E. Gladstone' 2
C. 'Lasurstern' 2	

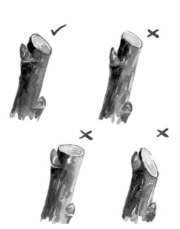

Pruning cuts

Correct cuts are very important to the health of all plants. Cuts should be sloping, just above a viable bud (top left).

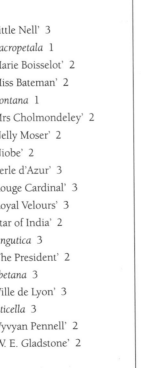

Wisteria

Wisteria needs to be pruned twice a year, once immediately after flowering and again in winter. Wisteria that has been allowed to run free without any pruning soon runs out of flower-power. In late summer, cut back all the new growth to four or five leaves. If you want to extend the plant's coverage, leave a few shoots to grow on. In winter, reduce the stems even further.

Late summer

Cut back all the new growth to 6 in (150 mm), or four or five leaves.

Winter

Cut back the stems even further, to 3–4 in (80–100 mm), or two to three buds.

Other climbers

A simple pruning regime can make all the difference to the performance of a climber, but it is vital to know if the plant flowers on old or new wood. Follow these guidelines: remove all dead, diseased, and dying wood; cut out a few of the older stems to promote new, vigorous growth; do not allow plants to become tangled. Climbers that flower on old wood should be pruned immediately after flowering; those that flower on new wood should be left until late winter or spring.

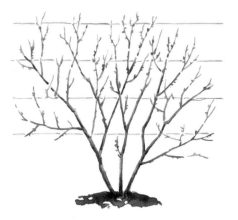

Plants that flower on new wood

Plants that flower on fresh growth should be pruned in late winter or early spring.

Plants that flower on old wood

These plants need pruning right after flowering so they have time to produce new shoots before winter.

Ways of attaching plants to structures

A variety of devices and structures can be attached to walls and fences to give plants support. Wires can be discreet, wooden trellis decorative, and, for smaller areas and plants that produce good leaf-cover, a rigid plastic mesh is effective (but unattractive, so it needs to be hidden).

For trellis, screw battens or blocks to the wall or fence (first drill holes into a wall with a masonry bit and use a plastic or masonry anchor plug); these will make it easier to weave stems behind the trellis and to tie them in.

Plastic mesh is attached using specially made clips that are screwed or nailed in place. The mesh can be unclipped to help pruning or maintenance of the supporting structure.

A YEAR IN THE HERB GARDEN

A plan for the year ahead in a herb garden should ideally be devised at the end of the growing season. This is because—except when heavy frosts occur—mid-fall is the best time to start planting a herb garden.

Mid-fall
• Container-grown plants can be planted at any time of year but will become established much better if they are planted in fall or spring. Water the plant thoroughly in its pot before planting. If you have a dry, bare-rooted plant, plunge the rootball into a bucket of water first.
• If you are planting a new herb bed on uncultivated ground, double dig the soil as described on page 250.
• Plant trees, shrubs, and hardy herbaceous herbs. Calculate how far apart they need to be planted based on their ultimate spread, and plant in groups of three, five, or seven depending on the space available.
• To prevent them from overwhelming neighboring plants, invasive herbs should be planted in a plastic bucket or similar container that can be sunk into the ground.
• Move tender herbs in containers into a greenhouse or conservatory.
• Grow parsley and marjoram in pots and overwinter indoors for a winter supply.
• Cut back larger shrubs.

Late fall
• Continue to plant bare-rooted trees and shrubs while the ground is free of frost. Plant low edging such as boxwood, hyssop, rue, and lavender, leaving about 9 in (230 mm) between each plant.
• If necessary, cover or mulch tender herbs for winter.

Early winter
• Remove soggy herbaceous and annual growth as the herbs die back but leave other growth undisturbed. This latter growth can provide useful protection for other plants during winter.
• Keep the herb garden neat, as you would in summer.

Midwinter
• Now is a good time to think about next year's planting. Order seeds and plan any alterations or improvements.

Late winter
• Towards the end of the season, sow the seed of tender herbs indoors.
• Plant pot-grown hardy herbaceous herbs and shrubs in frost-free weather.

Early spring
• Clear away all dead or herbaceous growth.
• Add a dressing of bonemeal to the ground and turn the soil with a fork.
• If the soil is not soggy, sow the first seed of hardy annuals and biennials.
• Be sure the ground is not too wet.
• Continue to plant hardy pot-grown herbs if the danger of frost has passed.

Mid-spring
• Plant container-grown herbs if required.
• Cut back shrubs such as lavender, sage, and santolina to keep them compact.
• Prune larger shrubs to shape.
• Continue to sow seed outdoors and to plant container-grown herbs.

- Apply an annual spring mulch of homemade compost or other organic fertilizer.
- Cut back Mediterranean shrubs such as rosemary and lavender to encourge compact new growth.
- Pinch out the growing ends of young shrubs to create a neat shape if required.
- Weed from mid-spring to early summer.

Late spring
- Move half-hardy and tender plants to a sheltered place so that they can be hardened off for an early summer planting.
- Beware of late frosts.
- Stake and support any trailing plants.

Early summer
- This is perhaps the best season in the herb garden, when the foliage looks particularly fresh and green. Many herbs will now be ready for harvesting.
- Trim dwarf hedges and formal plantings.

Midsummer
- Collect seed from early annuals and biennials for fall or spring sowing. Put the seed in separate envelopes and label them carefully.
- Harvest plants for drying and preserving.
- Collect rose petals and lavender flowers for potpourri and sachets.

Late summer
- Continue to collect petals and scented leaves from plants such as lemon verbena and scented geraniums and harvest herbs for drying and preserving.
- Collect seed as it ripens.
- Continue to cut formal hedges.

Early fall
- Dig up tender and half-hardy plants and move indoor to overwinter.
- Till the soil and fertilize any permanent planting.

Harvesting and drying
Harvest herbs on a dry, sunny morning after any moisture has evaporated from the leaves but before full sun. Handle aromatic herbs as little as possible to avoid bruising them and releasing the volatile oils. Foliage is usually harvested just before the appearance of the flowers, after which the foliage can become rather tough.

Small-leaved herbs should be dried in small bunches on the stem. Then remove the leaves and store in sealed containers. Whole flowers should be dried off the stalk, face upwards, on a tray lined with paper.

HERBS IN CONTAINERS

Among the advantages of growing herbs in containers is that culinary herbs in pots can be placed near the kitchen door for convenience of harvesting. Tender herbs can be moved indoors for the winter. You can also control the soil and growing conditions in a container far more easily than in a garden. For example, you can provide well-draining sandy soil or moist peaty soil for particular herbs. Many herbs enjoy the free-draining, dryish conditions that can easily be created by pot culture.

Planting containers
When planting your containers, make sure the planting medium is suitable for the type of herb you want to grow. In a mixed herb planting, it is important to consider how large the plants will eventually become and whether some may overwhelm others, although this can be corrected with pruning and annual division.

Check the moisture level of the soil in the containers every day. Water thoroughly from late spring throughout the growing season. The best time to water container-grown herbs is in the early morning or evening. Make sure that there is at least 1 in (25 mm) between the top of the soil and the rim of the pot in order to provide a watering reservoir. Feed the herb with a liquid fertilizer at least once every two weeks.

If your herbs become pot-bound—with roots protruding from the pot's base—repot in spring. Plant in a larger pot or divide the plant and repot into two or more pots.

useful addresses

PLANT SUPPLIERS AND NURSERIES

Andre Viette Farm & Nursery
994 Long Meadow Road
Fishersville, VA 22939
(800) 575-5538
www.viette.com
Perennials, with a special emphasis
on daylilies.

Avant Gardens
710 High Hill Road
Dartmouth, MA 02747
(508) 998-8819
www.avantgardensNE.com
A wide selection of plants.

Bluestone Perennials
7211 Middle Ridge Road
Madison, OH 44057
(800) 852-5243
www.bluestoneperennials.com
A wide array of perennials, plants,
herbs, ornamental shrubs, and bulbs.

Carroll Gardens
444 East Main Street
Westminster, MD 21157
(800) 638-6334
www.carrollgardens.com

Eastern Plant Specialties
P. O. Box 5692
Clark, NJ 07066
(732) 382-2508
www.easternplant.com
Native and woodland plants.

Glasshouse Works
Church Street
P. O. Box 97
Stewart, OH 45778
(800) 837-2142
www.rareplants.com
A nursery and showplace of
more than 10,000 species
of unique and rare plants.

Goodwin Creek Gardens
P .O. Box 83
Williams, OR 97544
(800) 846-7359
www.goodwincreekgardens.com
Heirlooms and contemporary cultivars;
useful and ornamental plants.

Heronswood Nursery
7530 NE 288th Street
Kingston, WA 98346
(360) 297-4172
www.heronswood.com
All types of plants; geared toward
the connoisseur and collector.

Logee's Greenhouses
141 North Street
Danielson, CT 06239
(888) 330-8038
www.logees.com
Tropical and subtropical plants.

McClure & Zimmerman
108 W. Winnebago Street
P. O. Box 368
Friesland, WI 53935
(800) 883-6998
www.mzbulb.com
Bulb specialist.

Wayside Gardens
1 Garden Lane
Hodges, SC 29695
(800) 213-0379
www.waysidegardens.com
Plants, perennials, and flowers.

White Flower Farm
P. O. Box 50, Route 63
Litchfield, CT 06759
(800) 503-9624
www.whiteflowerfarm.com
Perennials and some shrubs.

SPECIALISTS

Bamboo Sourcery
666 Wagnon Road
Sebastapol, CA 96472
(707) 823-5866
www.bamboosourcery.com

Completely Clematis
217 Argilla Road
Ipswich, MA 01938
(978) 356-3197
www.clematisnursery.com

Dutch Gardens
144 Intervale Road
Burlington, VT 05401
(888) 821-0448
www.dutchgardens.com
High-quality Holland bulbs.

Four Winds Growers
42186 Palm Avenue
Fremont, CA 94539
(510) 656-2591
www.fourwindsgrowers.com
Fruit trees; dwarf citrus, including
orange and lemon.

Hydrangeas Plus
P. O. Box 389
Aurora, OR 97002
(503) 651-2887
www.hydrangeasplus.com
Extensive hydrangea selection.

Lilypons Water Gardens
6800 Lily Pons Road
P. O. Box 10
Buckeystown, MD 21717
(800) 999-5459
www.lilypons.com
Tropical lilies and lotus, and other
water gardening supplies.

Miller Nurseries
5060 West Lake Road
Canandaigua, NY 14424
(800) 836-9630
www.millernurseries.com
Fruit and nut trees, berries, grapes,
and much more.

Plant Delights Nursery
9241 Sauls Road
Raleigh, NC 27603
(919) 772-4794
www.plantdelights.com
An amazing selection of hostas. Plus
tropicals, and bog and acquatic plants.

ROSES

Antique Rose Emporium
9300 Lueckmeyer Road
Brenham, TX 77833
(800) 441-0002
www.antiqueroseemporium.com
Antique roses.

David Austin Roses Limited
15059 Highway 64 West
Tyler, TX 75704
(903) 526-1800
www.davidaustionroses.com
The authority on award-winning
English roses.

Edmunds' Roses
6235 SW Kahle Road
Wilsonville, OR 97070
(888) 481-7673
www.edmundsroses.com
Modern roses, specializing in European
and exhibition varieties.

Jackson & Perkins
1 Rose Lane
Medford, OR 97501
(877) 322-2300
www.jacksonandperkins.com
100 varieties of premium-quality roses

HERBS

Catnip Acres Herb Nursery
(Our Grandmother's Garden)
67 Christian Street
Oxford, CT 06478
(203) 888-5649
www.ourgrandmothersgarden.com
Herb plants and seeds, botanicals,
and blends.

Companion Plants
7247 North Coolville Ridge Road
Athens, OH 45701
(740) 592-4643
www.companionplants.com
Common and unusual seeds, herbs,
and mushrooms.

Rasland Herb Farm
NC 82 at US 13
Godwin, NC 28344
(910) 567-2705
Everything herbal, including plants.
Phone ahead for a tour.

Sandy Mush Herb Nursery
316 Surrett Cove Road
Leicester, NC 28748
(828) 683-2014
www.sandymushherbs.com
A vast selection of varying herbs
and perennials.

The Thyme Garden Herb Company
20546 Alsea Highway
Alsea, OR 97324
(541) 487-8671
www.thymegarden.com
Herbs from the common to the exotic.

VEGETABLE AND FLOWER SEEDS

Burpee's
W. Atlee Burpee Seed Co.
300 Park Avenue
Warminster, PA 18974
(800) 888-1447
www.burpee.com

The Cook's Garden
P. O. Box 5030
Warminster, PA 18974
(800) 547-9703
www.cooksgarden.com
Seed company for market gardeners.

Gurney's Seed & Nursery Co.
P. O. Box 4178
Greendale, IN 47025
(513) 354-1491
www.gurneys.com

Johnny's Selected Seeds
955 Benton Avenue
Winslow, ME 04901
(207) 861-3900
www.johnnyseeds.com
Huge selection of seeds, including
chiles and tomatoes.

Nichols Garden Nursery
1190 Old Salem Road NE
Albany, OR 97321
(800) 422-3985
www.nicholsgardennursery.com
Seed company offering a variety
of Asian vegetable seeds.

Park's Gardens
1 Parkton Avenue
Greenwood, SC 29647
(800) 213-0076
www.parkseed.com
Flowers, vegetables, and information.

Peaceful Valley Farm
P. O. Box 2209
125 Clydesdale Court
Grass Valley, CA 95945
(888) 784-1722
www.groworganic.com
Organic gardening and farming supplies,
from seed to tools.

Seeds of Change
P. O. Box 15700
Santa Fe, NM 87506
(888) 762-7333
www.seedsofchange.com
Organic seeds and food products.

Select Seeds
180 Stickney Hill Road
Union, CT 06076
(800) 684-0395
www.selectseeds.com
Rare and old-fashioned flower varieties.

MATERIALS AND TOOLS

Ace Hardware Corporation
2200 Kensington Court
Oak Brook, IL 60523
(866) 290-5334
www.acehardware.com
Hardware from A to Z with seasonal
gardening supplies.

Agway, Inc.
A division of Southern States
P. O. Box 26234
Richmond, VA 23260
(804) 281-1000
www.agway.com
Agriculture, farm, and garden products.

The Home Depot
(800) 430-3376
www.homedepot.com
Chain store with home and garden
supplies and materials.

Lowe's
Located throughout the U.S.A.
(800) 445-6937
www.Lowes.com
A nationwide chain warehouse of
home improvement supplies.

GARDEN SUPPLIES

Dan's Garden Shop
5821 Woodwinds Circle
Frederick, MD 21703
Fax (301) 662-3572
www.dansgardenshop.com

Gardener's Supply Company
128 Intervale Road
Burlington, VT 05401
(888) 833-1412
www.gardeners.com
Tools, containers, soil, seed, and
everything to garden, including
flower supports and bamboo.

Home Harvest Garden Supply
A division of Superior Growers Supply
4870 Dawn Avenue
East Lansing, MI 48823
(800) 227-0027
www.homeharvest.com
Wide variety and selection, with
lots of pots.

Kinsman Company
River Road
Point Pleasant, PA 18950
(800) 733-4146
www.kinsmangarden.com
Classy garden items, including moss-
lined baskets and troughs.

Kmart
(866) 562-7848
www.kmart.com
Chain store with locations throughout
the U.S.A. Gardening supplies and
seasonal flowers.

LaBrake's Garden Path and Pond
8 Pitt Street
Brushton, NY 12916
(877) 909-5459
www.gardenponds.com

Smith and Hawken
P. O. Box 8690
Pueblo, CO 81008
(800) 940-1170
www.smith-hawken.com
Mail-order supplier of garden supplies,
ornaments, and specialties. Catalog
includes English rose arches.

Walt Nicke's Garden Talk
P. O. Box 433
Topsfield, MA 01983
(978) 887-3388
www.gardentalk.com
Fine tools and garden ornaments.

CONTAINERS

Brooks Barrel Company
5228 Bucktown Road
P. O. Box 1056
Cambridge, MD 21613
(800) 398-2766
www.brooksbarrel.com
Handcrafted wooden barrels, kegs,
and planters of all sizes.

Master Garden Products
3223 C Street NE #1
Auburn, WA 98002
(800) 574-7248
www.mastergardenproducts.com
Teak tubs and barrels.

Windowbox.com
3821 South Santa Fe Avenue
Vernon, CA 90058
(888) GARDEN-Box
www.windowbox.com
Especially for the rooftop or balcony
gardener. Unusual planters and plenty
of online advice.

CRAFTS

Ben Franklin
Nationwide franchises.
(800) 992-9307
www.benfranklinstores.com
Craft supplies galore, including
differing sizes of pine cones.

Michael's Stores
8000 Bent Branch Drive
Irving, TX 75063
(800) 642-4235
www.michaels.com
An arts and crafts store with a great
selection. Good source for metal leaf.

Target
33 South Sixth Street
Minneapolis, MN 55402
(800) 440-0680
www.target.com
Modern variety store with craft needs
and slightly sophisticated plastic.

credits

The authors and publishers would like to thank the people and organizations named below for their contributions to this book.

The garden owners and designers who allowed their gardens to be photographed: Belinda Barnes and Ronald Stuart-Moonlight (Rommany Road, London); Jonathan and Sam Buckley (Barry Road, London); Mr and Mrs David Cargill; Ethne Clarke; Mr and Mrs Robert Clarke; Mike Crosby Jones (Gopsall Pottery, Winchelsea, Sussex); Mr and Mrs Collum (Clinton Lodge, Sussex); Viscount and Viscountess De L'Isle; Mr and Mrs Jeffrey Eker (Old Place Farm, Kent); Gordon Fenn and Raymond Treasure (Stockton Bury, Herts); Major and Mrs Charles Fenwick; Wendy Francis (The Anchorage, West Wickham, Kent); Mrs Clive Hardcastle; Simon and Judith Hopkinson (Hollington Nurseries, Berks); Mr and Mrs Derek Howard; Rosemary Lindsay (Burbage Road, London); Christopher Lloyd (Great Dixter, East Sussex); Janie Lloyd Owen (Eglatine Road, London); Mrs Macleod-Matthews (Chenies Manor, Bucks); Sue Martin (Frittenden, Kent); Dr and Mrs Mitchell (Warren Farm Cottages, Hants); Mr and Mrs Mogford (Rofford Manor, Oxon); David and Mavis Seeney (The Herb Farm, Reading, Berks); The Lady Tollemache; Julian Upston (Cinque Cottage, Ticehurst, East Sussex); Mr and Mrs Williams (Marle Place, Kent); Mr and Mrs Richard Winch; Helen Yemm (Brodrick Road, London).

The owners or managers of: Axletree Garden and Nursery, Peasmarsh, East Sussex; Bates Green, Arlington, East Sussex; Beth Chatto Gardens, Elmstead Market, Essex; Grace Barrand Design Centre, Nutfield, Surrey; The Chelsea Physic Garden, London; Terence Conran's Chef's Garden, RHS Flower Show, Chelsea; Hadspen Garden and Nursery, Castle Cary, Somerset; Hailsham Grange, Hailsham, East Sussex; Hatfield House, Herts; Holkham Hall Garden Centre, Holkham, Norfolk; King John's Lodge, Etchingham, East Sussex; Long Barn, Kent; Marle Place, Brenchley, Kent; Merriments Garden, Hurst Green, East Sussex; Queen Anne's, Goudhurst, Kent; RHS Gardens, Wisley; Royal Botanic Gardens, Kew; Snape Cottage, Chaffeymoor, Dorset; Sticky Wicket Garden, Buckland Newton, Dorset; Upper Mill Cottage, Loose, Kent; West Dean Gardens, Sussex (Edward James Foundation); Whole Earth Foods, Portobello Road, London; Wyland Wood, Robertsbridge, East Sussex.

The photographs on pages 76–77 center, 94, and 95 were taken by Clive Nichols (Potager-style herb garden with lemon balm in terra cotta pot, Chelsea 1993, National Asthma Campaign garden).

Photographs by Jonathan Buckley: pages 5 center, 7, 8–9 center, 86, 87, 124, 125, 164 left, 164–165 center, 166, 167, 174, 175, 178, 179, 182, 183, 194–195 all, 196, 197, 200, 201, 204, 205, 208, 209, 220, 221, 224, 225, 228, 229, 232, 233, 236, 237, 240, 241.

Photographs by Marianne Majerus: pages 2, 5 above and below, 8 left, 9 right, 10, 11, 14, 15, 18, 19, 22, 23, 26, 27, 30, 31, 34, 35, 38, 39, 42, 43, 46–47 all, 48, 49, 52, 53, 56, 57, 60, 61, 64, 65, 68, 69, 72, 73, 77 right, 78, 79, 82, 83, 106 left, 107 right, 116, 117, 120, 121, 128, 129, 144, 145, 148, 149, 152, 153, 156, 157, 190, 191, 212, 213.

Photographs by Stephen Robson: pages 76 left, 90, 91, 98, 99, 102, 103, 106–107 center, 108, 109, 112, 113, 132, 133, 136, 137, 140, 141, 160, 161, 165 right, 170, 171, 186, 187, 216, 217.

index

A

Acaena, 172
Acanthus mollis, 13
Achillea clavennae, 173
   A. millefolium 'Cerise Queen', 235
adhesives, 245
aging containers, 254
Ajuga reptans 'Atropurpurea', 41
Alchemilla alpina, 170, 172
   A. conjuncta, 170, 172
   A. mollis, 60, 189, 235
Allium schoenoprasum, 41, 81, 119, 151, 215, 235
   A. tuberosum, 81, 235
Aloysia triphylla, 186
Althaea officinalis, 235
aluminum leaf, shell-faced trough, 48–51
Androsace carnea subsp. *laggeri*, 173
Anemone x *hybrida*, 235
Anethum graveolens, 81
Angelica archangelica, 235
annuals: planting, 251
   sowing, 252
Anthemis nobile 'Treneague', 63
   A. tinctoria 'Sauce Hollandaise', 101
Anthriscus cerefolium, 215
aphids, 255
apple trees, 211, 219
Aptenia cordifolia 'Variegata', 48
arbors: bean arbor, 240–3
   scented arbor, 124–7
arch, rose, 160–3
Argyranthemum frutescens, 10, 13, 21
Armeria formosa, 101
   A. juniperifolia, 173
Artemisia, 186
   A. absinthium, 41
   A. caucasica, 189
   A. dracunculus, 81, 119, 235
   A. 'Powys Castle', 42
Asian vegetables, 228–31
Aster alpinus, 173
   A. ericoides 'Blue Star', 101
   A. x *frikartii*, 235
   A. novi-belgii 'Marie Ballard', 101
Astrantia major, 235
Athyrium filix-femina, 120
   A. f. cristatum, 56
atriplex, red, 239
Atriplex hortensis 'Rubra', 216, 218
Aubrieta 'Joy', 173
   A. 'Triumphante', 101

Aucuba japonica, 25
azaleas, 186

B

balcony herb boxes, 38–41
barrels, culinary herb half-barrels, 212–15
basil, 41, 215
   purple basil, 29, 215
baskets of tomatoes, 196–9
bay, 97, 235
   golden bay, 215
beans: bean arbor, 240–3
   bush beans, 89
   green beans, 219
   pole beans, 89
   runner beans, 207, 240–3
bear's breeches, 13
beets, 89, 207, 223
bellflowers, 52
Benomyl, 255
Berberis, 186
bird pests, 227
black spot, 255
blackfly, 255
blanching celery, 223
blueberries, 211
board surrounds, strawberry beds, 227
bonds, brickwork, 248–9
Borago officinalis (borage), 41, 219, 235
borders: edible border, 216–19
   herb border, 232–5
   maintenance, 256–7
   planning, 251
boundaries, solid, 248–9
boxwood, 13, 21, 68, 85, 116, 118, 226, 238
   silver boxwood, 116
brickwork projects, 77
   bonds, 248–9
   brick-edged herb garden, 78–81
   brickwork trough, 82–5
   cold frames, 228–31
   herb-lined pathway, 94–7
   potagers, 238
   raised beds, 86–93, 249
   wall cascade, 102–5
   walls, 248–9
brushes, paint, 244
buckets, galvanized, 42–5
bugle, bronze, 41
bulbs, planting, 253
Buxus sempervirens, 13, 21, 68, 85, 116, 118
   B. s. 'Elegantissima', 116

   B. s. 'Suffruticosa', 224–7
buying plants, 253

C

cabbages, 89
Calaminta grandiflora, 235
calamondin orange, 211
Calendula officinalis, 42, 215, 216, 218
Camellia, 255
   C. japonica, 13
   C. j. 'Alba Plena', 159
camouflage box, wood and trellis, 10–13
Campanula carpatica, 52, 173
canes: rose growing through a tree, 185
   sweet pea obelisk, 174–7
cardoons, 216, 218, 235, 239
Carissa grandiflora, 211
carrots, 89, 207, 219
Caryopteris incana, 101
celery, 89, 223
   Japanese celery, 231
Chamaemelum nobile, 30, 33
   C. n. 'Treneague', 168
chamomile, 63
   chamomile seat, 30–3
checkerboard parterre, 144–7
cherry pie heliotrope, 48
chervil, 215
chestnut poles, 227
chile peppers in pots, 200–3
chives, 41, 81, 119, 151, 189, 215, 235, 239
Choisya ternata, 186
choy sum, 231
chrysanthemums, 42, 85, 123, 231
circular pipe with flowering tree, 60–3
Citrofortunella microcarpa, 211
Citrus limon 'Variegata', 211
   C. meyeri 'Meyer', 211
Clematis, 108, 111, 128, 182, 257, 258
   C. 'Abundance', 258
   C. alpina, 258
   C. armandii, 258
   C. 'Barbara Dibley', 258
   C. 'Barbara Jackman', 258
   C. 'Bill MacKenzie', 258
   C. cirrhosa, 258
   C. 'Comtesse de Bouchaud', 258
   C. 'Countess of Lovelace', 258
   C. 'Daniel Deronda', 258
   C. 'Doctor Ruppel', 258
   C. 'Duchess of Albany', 258
   C. 'Elsa Späth', 258

C. 'Ernest Markham', 258
C. 'Etoile Violette', 258
C. 'Gipsy Queen', 258
C. 'Hagley Hybrid', 258
C. 'H.F. Young', 258
C. 'Jackmanii', 258
C. 'Lasurstern', 258
C. 'Little Nell', 258
C. macropetala, 258
C. 'Marie Boisselot', 258
C. 'Miss Bateman', 258
C. 'Mrs Cholmondeley', 258
C. montana, 182, 258
C. 'Nelly Moser', 258
C. 'Niobe', 258
C. 'Perle d'Azur', 111, 258
C. 'The President', 115, 258
C. 'Rouge Cardinal', 258
C. 'Royal Velours', 258
C. 'Star of India', 258
C. tangutica, 258
C. texensis, 111
C. tibetana, 258
C. 'Ville de Lyon', 258
C. viticella, 258
C. 'Vyvyan Pennell', 258
C. 'W.E. Gladstone', 258
climbing plants: bean arbor, 240–3
  fixing to structures, 259
  honeysuckle porch, 178–81
  pergolas, 219
  planting, 255
  pruning, 257–9
  rose arch, 160–3
  rose growing through a tree, 182–5
  rustic trellis, 112–15
  scented arbor, 124–7
  sweet pea obelisk, 174–7
  trellis, 108–11
  trough with trellis screen, 22–5
cold frames, 228–31
compost, garden, 250
composts, for containers, 254
concrete, mixing, 248
concrete pipes, circular pipe with flowering
  tree, 60–3
cone flowers, 42
containers, 9–75
  balcony herb boxes, 38–41
  basic window box, 246
  brickwork trough, 82–5
  care and maintenance, 254–5
  chamomile seat, 30–3
  chile peppers in pots, 200–3
  choosing, 254
  circular pipe with flowering tree, 60–3
  culinary herb half-barrels, 212–15
  decorated containers, 47–75

entrance containers, 18–21
  fruit trees in pots, 208–11
  galvanized buckets, 42–5
  herbal window box, 26–9
  herbs in, 261
  lead-faced trough, 52–5
  painted galvanized washtub, 64–7
  painted pots, 72–5
  patio container garden, 204–7
  planting, 254–5
  potagers, 239
  raised scented window box, 34–7
  rustic window box, 56–9
  shell-faced trough, 48–51
  sweet peas, 177
  terra cotta with a patina, 68–71
  trough with trellis screen, 22–5
  Versailles case, 14–17
  vertical planting, 120–3
  wood and trellis camouflage box, 10–13
  wooden obelisk, 128–31
Convallaria majalis, 186
Convolvulus althaeoides, 173
  C. sabatius, 51
Coreopsis tinctoria, 45
corn, 219
corner planting, 170–3
corners, mitered, 247
Corylus maxima 'Purpurea', 93
cos lettuce, 223
cottage-style gardens, 189
Crataegus monogyna, 128
creeping soft grass, 68
crested female ferns, 56
cucumbers, 223
cup flowers, 56
curry plant, 41, 119
curved picket fences, 139
Cynara cardunculus, 216, 218, 235

D
Daphne, 186
  D. odorata 'Aureomarginata', 13
  D. tangutica, 173
daylilies, 216, 218
deadheading, 256
decorated containers, 47–75
Delphinium, 256
  D. belladonna 'Wendy', 48
Deschampsia flexuosa, 170, 172
Dianthus, 186
  D. 'Annabel', 173
  D. 'Gran's Favorite', 189
  D. 'Haytor White', 189
  D. 'Laced Monarch', 189
  D. 'Little Jock', 173
  D. 'Mrs Sinkins', 235
  D. 'Terry Sutcliffe', 101

Diascia vigilis 'Jack Elliott', 101
digging, 250
dill, 81
diseases, 255
doors, rose arches, 163
double digging, 250
drainage: culinary herb half-barrels, 214
  raised beds, 88, 92, 249
  retaining walls, 100, 101
drying herbs, 261
Dryopteris filix-mas, 56

E
Echium creticum 'Blue Bedder', 119
edgings: miniature hurdles, 132–5
  potagers, 238
  wirework basket, 156–9
edible border, 216–19
English bond, brickwork, 248
entrance containers, 18–21
Epilobium angustifolium 'Album', 235
equipment, 244–5
Erigeron, 172
Erinus alpinus, 173
Erodium corsicum, 173
  E. manescaui, 101
Erysimum, 186
Euonymus fortunei 'Kewensis', 85
Euphorbia dulcis 'Chameleon', 101
  E. lathyris, 101
  E. myrsinites, 173
  E. stricta, 170, 172
evening primroses, 235
Exacum affine, 52
eyesores, screens, 143

F
fall care, perennials, 257
fences: picket fences, 136–9
  trellis-enclosed herb garden, 116–19
  trellis fence panel, 247
  wattle panels, 140–3
fennel, 235
  bronze fennel, 41, 81, 214
  Florence fennel, 239
ferns, 56, 120
fertilizers, 251
  borders, 256
  chile peppers, 203
  containers, 255
  fruit trees, 210
  hanging baskets, 199
  herbs, 261
feverfew, golden, 41
finials: picket fences, 139
  pine cone, 59
  trellis, 111
Flemish bond, brickwork, 249

flowers: deadheading, 256
  edible flowers, 218
  see also scented plants
Foeniculum vulgare, 235
  F. v. 'Purpureum', 41, 81, 214
forget-me-nots, 123
foundations: brickwork trough, 84
  cold frames, 230
  concrete, 248
  raised beds, 92, 249
  retaining walls, 100
  wall cascade, 104
Fragaria vesca, 97
French beans, 219
frost protection: containers, 254
  exotic fruit trees, 211
fruit: fruit trees in pots, 208–11
  strawberry bed, 224–7
Fuchsia x *speciosa* 'La Bianca', 13, 60–3
fungal diseases, 255

G
galvanized buckets, 42–5
galvanized washtub, painted, 64–7
garden centers, 253
garland chrysanthemum, 231
garlic chives, 81, 235
Gazania 'Orange Beauty', 45
Gentiana septemfida, 173
Geranium, 256
  G. cinereum subsp. *subcaulescens*, 173
  G. dalmaticum, 101
  G. phaeum, 235
  G. pratense 'Mrs Kendall Clark', 170, 172
  G. sanguineum 'Album', 189
geranium, scented, 235
gingermint, 215
  variegated gingermint, 97
glass, cold frames, 231
glues, 245
gooseberries, 207, 211
grapes, 219
gravel: bean arbor, 242
  brick-edged herb garden, 78
  checkerboard parterre, 147
  corner planting, 172
  herb border, 234
  potagers, 238
greenfly, 255

H
half-barrels, culinary herbs, 212–15
hammers, 244
hanging baskets, tomatoes, 196–9
hardwood, 245
harvesting herbs, 261
hawthorn, 25, 128, 131
hazel poles: hoops, 135

strawberry beds, 227
heartsease, 151, 215, 219
Hebe pinguifolia 'Pagei', 82, 85
  H. salicifolia, 101
Hedera helix, 25, 67, 120
  H. h. 'Erecta', 13
hedges: scented knot garden, 166–9
  strawberry bed, 224–7
  windbreaks, 143
Helianthemum 'Annabel', 173
  H. 'Rhodanthe Carneum', 101
Helianthus, 45
  H. annuus, 216, 218
Helichrysum italicum, 41, 119
Heliotropium peruvianum 'Royal Marine', 48
Hemerocallis, 216, 218
herbicides, 257
herbs: balcony herb boxes, 38–41
  brick-edged herb garden, 78–81
  checkerboard parterre, 144–7
  in containers, 261
  culinary herb half-barrels, 212–15
  herb border, 232–5
  herb-lined pathway, 94–7
  herb staging, 148–51
  herb topiary, 190–3
  herbal window box, 26–9
  patio container garden, 204–7
  planting, 261
  raised scented window box, 34–7
  trellis-enclosed herb garden, 116–19
  a year in the herb garden, 260–1
Hesperis matronalis, 186
Heuchera macrantha 'Palace Purple', 93
Holcus mollis 'Albovariegatus', 68
holly, 25, 85, 169
honeysuckle, 108, 116, 118, 128, 182, 257
  honeysuckle porch, 178–81
hoops, hazel, 135
hops, 128, 215
horsemint, 119
Humulus lupulus, 215
hurdles: miniature hurdles, 132–5
  strawberry beds, 227
  wattle panels, 140–3
Hyacinthus, 85, 186
Hydrangea macrophylla, 18
Hypericum olympicum 'Citrinum', 173
hyssop, 239

I
Ilex aquifolium, 169
  I. a. 'Silver Queen', 168
  I. foetidissima, 235
  I. x *meserveae* 'Blue Prince', 85
  I. unguicularis, 186
ivy, 13, 67, 85, 120, 123, 128, 196, 257

J
jasmine, 180
Juniperus communis 'Compressa', 173

K
kale, flowering, 85
Kew wintercreeper, 85
knot garden, scented, 166–9

L
lady's mantle, 60, 235, 256
lamb's ears, 119
Lathyrus odoratus, 174, 186, 235
Laurentia axillaris 'Blue Star', 48
Laurus nobilis, 97, 235
  L. n. 'Aurea', 215
Lavandula, 186–9
  L. angustifolia, 81, 116, 118, 119, 235
  L. a. 'Hidcote', 37
  L. 'Sawyers', 37
  L. stoechas pedunculata, 235
lavender, 37, 186–9, 235, 239
  English lavender, 81, 116, 118, 119
lead-faced trough, 52–5
leaf spot, 255
leeks, 89, 207, 239
lemon balm, 207, 235
  golden lemon balm, 41, 97
lemon thyme, 97
  golden lemon thyme, 151
lemon trees, 211, 255
lemon verbena, 207
Leptospermum scoparium, 14
lettuces, 89, 199, 207, 219, 222, 223, 239
Levisticum officinale, 29, 235
Lewisia tweedyi, 173
lights, cold frames, 230–1
Lilium (lilies), 72, 186
  L. candidum, 75
  L. 'Reinesse', 72, 75
linden, red-twigged, 120–3
liners: containers, 254
  hanging baskets, 198
  wall cascade, 104
loam-based composts, 254
Lonicera periclymenum, 116
  L. similis delavayi, 178
lovage, 29, 235
lumber, 245
Lupinus, 186
  L. 'Kayleigh Ann Savage', 189
Lychnis flos-jovis, 101

M
mail-order plants, 253
male ferns, 56
marguerites, 10, 13, 21
marigolds: African marigolds, 42

pot marigolds, 42, 215
marjoram, 119, 151, 206, 207
    golden marjoram, 41, 81, 97, 151
    wild marjoram, 41, 151
marsh mallow, 235
Matthiola, 186
Melissa officinalis, 235
    M. o. 'Aurea', 41, 97
Mentha, 186, 219
    M. x *gracilis*, 215
    M. x *gracilis* 'Variegata', 97
    M. x *longifolia*, 119
    M. x *piperita*, 41
    M. x *piperita* 'Citrata', 29, 151
    M. spicata, 151, 235
    M. suaveolens 'Variegata', 151
metalwork, 107
    bean arbor, 240–3
    rose arch, 160–3
    tools, 245
    wirework basket, 156–9
Meyer's lemon, 211
Mimulus guttatus, 170, 172
miniature hurdles, 132–5
mint, 172, 189, 219, 235
    apple mint, 239
    Eau de cologne mint, 29, 151
    pineapple mint, 151
    spearmint, 151
mitered corners, 247
mizuma greens, 239
Monarda didyma, 186
Morus alba 'Pendula', 63
mulberry, weeping, 63
mulches, 252
    for containers, 255
    strawberry bed, 226
mustard greens, 231
Myosotis alpestris, 123
Myrrhis odorata, 235
myrtle, 41
    creeping, 22
Myrtus communis, 41, 186

N
nasturtiums, 151, 215, 219
Natal plum, 211
Nemesia caerulea, 52
Nepeta, 256
    N. x *faassenii*, 115, 235
    N. govaniana, 235
    N. sibirica, 235
netting: strawberry beds, 227
    supports, 256
Nicotiana, 186
    N. alata 'Lime Green', 82, 85
    N. Domino Series, 64
    N. 'Domino White', 168

nicotine, 255
Nierembergia, 56
nurseries, buying plants, 253

O
obelisks: sweet pea obelisk, 174–7
    wooden obelisk, 128–31
Ocimum basilicum, 41, 215
    O. b. purpurascens, 29, 215
Oenothera biennis, 235
orache, red, 216, 218
orange trees, 255
oregano, 29, 41, 97, 235
    Greek oregano, 119
organic matter, improving soil, 250
organic mulches, 252
Origanum, 186
    O. onites, 119
    O. vulgare, 29, 41, 97, 119, 151, 235
    O. v. 'Aureum', 41, 81, 97, 151
    O. v. 'Country Cream', 41
    O. v. 'Gold Tip', 151
Osmanthus, 186
Osteospermum 'Buttermilk', 72, 75
    O. 'Whirly Gig', 52

P
paints, 245
    brushes, 244
    painted galvanized washtub, 64–7
    painted pots, 72–5
pak choi, 231
pansies, 51, 193
paraffin, 255
parsley, 29, 41, 81, 89, 215, 235
    curly-leaved parsley, 151, 239
    flat-leaved parsley, 239
    French parsley, 29, 41, 214
parsnips, 89
parterre, checkerboard, 144–7
paths: herb border, 234
    herb-lined pathway, 94–7
    pergolas, 219
    potagers, 238
    rose arch, 163
    scented path, 186–9
patio container garden, 204–7
patio roses, 207
paving slabs: herb border, 234
    herb-lined pathway, 94–7
    patio container garden, 206
    potagers, 238
pea gravel, checkerboard parterre, 147
pea-stick supports, 256
pears, 207, 219
peas, 219
peat-based composts, 254
Pelargonium 'Friesdorf', 60

P. graveolens, 235
Penstemon 'Mother of Pearl', 101
peppermint, 41
peppers, 203
perennials: maintaining borders, 256–7
    sowing, 252
pergolas, 219
permethrin, 255
Persian violets, 52
pests, 255
    birds, 227
    salad crops, 223
Petroselinum crispum, 29, 235
    P. c. 'Italian', 29, 41, 214
    P. c. 'Moss Curled', 41, 81, 151, 215
Petunia, 72, 75, 120, 123
    P. 'Dark Blue Dwarf', 22
    P. 'Purple', 196, 198
    P. 'Ruby', 52
Phaseolus coccineus, 240
Philadelphus, 186
    P. 'Sybille', 235
Phillyrea angustifolia, 116, 118
Phlox douglasii 'Crackerjack', 173
Phormium tenax 'Purpureum', 93
Picea mariana 'Nana', 173
picket fences, 136–9
pine cone finials, 59
pipes, circular pipe with flowering tree, 60–3
pirimicarb, 255
planning borders, 251
planting, 251
    bulbs, 253
    containers, 254–5
    herbs, 261
    seedlings, 253
plastic mesh, supporting climbing plants, 259
plastic mulches, 252
plastic pots, 210
pleaching linden trees, 122
Plectranthus coleoides 'Variegatus', 196
plywood, 245
pole cage, rose growing through a tree, 185
Polygala chamaebuxus var. *grandiflora*, 173
poppies, 256
porch, honeysuckle, 178–81
potagers, 236–9
potatoes, 207
pots: chile peppers in pots, 200–3
    fruit trees in pots, 208–11
    painted pots, 72–5
    in potagers, 239
    sowing seeds in, 253
potting on, fruit trees, 210
powdery mildew, 255
preservatives, wood, 245

pricking out seedlings, 253
Primula denticulata, 152
  P. Gold Lace Group, 152
  P. veris, 152
  P. vulgaris, 152
primula theater, 152–5
pruning, 257–9
Pulsatilla vulgaris, 173
pumps, wall cascade, 105
Pyracantha coccinea, 25

R
radicchio, 223
radishes, 222, 223, 239
railroad ties, raised beds, 92, 93, 249
raised beds, 249
  raised brick bed, 86–9
  raised brick flower bed, 90–3
raised scented window box, 34–7
rambling roses, 182
  pruning, 257
Repton, Humphrey, 56
Reseda odorata, 186
retaining walls, 98–101
Rhododendron, 186
Rhodohypoxis baurii, 173
rhubarb, 239
rock gardens, corner planting, 170–3
roses, 180, 186
  edible border, 219
  growing through a tree, 182–5
  patio roses, 207
  potagers, 239
  pruning, 257
  rose arch, 160–3
  on trellis, 108
  Rosa 'Adélaïde d'Orléans', 115, 160, 162
  R. 'The Fairy', 156
  R. 'Félicité et Perpétue', 182, 239
  R. 'Fragrant Cloud', 168
  R. 'Ispahan', 101
  R. 'Marguerite Hilling', 159
  R. 'Nevada', 159
  R. 'New Dawn', 124–7
  R. 'Nozomi', 159
  R. 'Sanders' White Rambler', 82, 85
  R. 'White Pet', 101, 159
Rosmarinus (rosemary), 29, 37, 119, 144–7, 151, 186, 190–3, 207, 211, 215, 219, 235, 239
ruby chard, 239
Rudbeckia hirta, 42
rue, 41, 235
  variegated rue, 41
runner beans, 207, 240–3
running bond, brickwork, 249
rustic picket fences, 139
rustic trellis, 112–15

rustic window box, 56–9
Ruta graveolens, 235
  R. g. 'Jackman's Blue', 41
  R. g. 'Variegata', 41
rutabaga, 89

S
sage, 29, 41, 81, 119, 151, 189, 207, 235, 239
  purple sage, 81, 97, 151, 214
  tangerine sage, 215
salads: hanging baskets, 199
  salad bed, 220–3
Salvia elegans, 215
  S. officinalis, 41, 81, 119, 151, 186
  S. o. 'Icterina', 29, 41, 119, 151, 235
  S. o. Purpurascens Group, 81, 97, 151, 214
  S. x superba, 115
Santolina, 168–9
  S. chamaecyparissus 'Lambrook Silver', 168
  S. c. nana, 168
  S. pinnata neapolitana, 168
  S. p. n. 'Sulphurea', 168
  S. rosmarinifolia, 168
Sarcococca, 186
Satureja hortensis, 97, 151, 215
  S. montana, 119, 235
savory: summer savory, 97, 151, 215
  winter savory, 119, 235
saws, 244
scale insects, 255
scallop shells, shell-faced trough, 48–51
scented plants: honeysuckle porch, 178–81
  raised scented window box, 34–7
  roses growing through trees, 182–5
  scented arbor, 124–7
  scented knot garden, 166–9
  scented path, 186–9
screens: wattle panels, 143
  see also trellis
screw eyes, 180
screwdrivers, 244
screws, 245
seat, chamomile, 30–3
Sedum acre, 214
seedlings, pricking out, 253
seeds, 252–3
  chile peppers, 202
  salad crops, 222
  sweet peas, 176
Senecio cineraria, 52
shell-faced trough, 48–51
shrubs: in containers, 255
  planting, 251
  pruning, 257
  staking, 256
Sisyrinchium subsp. *bellum*, 173
sloping sites, retaining walls, 98–101

slugs, 223
soil: mulches, 252
  planning borders, 251
  preparation, 250
sorrel, French, 239
sowing, 252–3
  chile pepper seeds, 202
  salad crops, 222
  sweet pea seeds, 176
spearmint, 151
spring onions, 223
squashes, 219, 239
Stachys byzantina 'Silver Carpet', 119
staging: chile peppers in pots, 203
  herb staging, 148–51
  primula theater, 152–5
stains, wood, 245
staking, 256
stepping stones, 234
steps, rose arch, 163
stonecrop, 214
stonework, 77
  raised brick flower bed, 93
  retaining walls, 98–101
straw mulches, 226
strawberries, 207
  alpine (wild) strawberries, 89, 97, 239
  strawberry bed, 224–7
  strawberry pots, 206–7, 211
summer savory, 151, 215
sunflowers, 216, 218
  dwarf sunflowers, 45
supports: for climbing plants, 259
  netting, 256
  pea-sticks, 256
  string and stakes, 256
Swedish ivy, variegated, 196
sweet chestnut hurdles, 132–5
sweet Cicely, 235
sweet peas, 235, 239
  sweet pea obelisk, 174–7
Swiss chard, 219
Syringa, 186

T
Tagetes erecta, 42
Tanacetum parthenium 'Aureum', 41, 189, 235
tarragon, 239
  French tarragon, 81, 119, 235
tea tree, New Zealand, 14
terra cotta: chile peppers in pots, 200–3
  fruit trees in pots, 208–11
  painted pots, 72–5
  patio container garden, 204–7
  potagers, 239
  terra cotta with a patina, 68–71
texsel greens, 231

theater, primula, 152–5
thyme, 29, 80, 119, 172, 189, 206, 219, 235
  creeping thyme, 81
  golden thyme, 214
  lemon thyme, 214
  silver thyme, 37, 41, 81
  white thyme, 214
  wild thyme, 41
Thymus x *citriodorus* 'Archer's Gold', 214
  T. x *citriodorus* 'Aureus', 151
  T. x *citriodorus* 'Bertram Anderson', 97
  T. polytrichus, 81
  T. serpyllum, 235
  T. s. 'Lemon Curd', 41
  T. vulgaris, 29, 81, 119
  T. v. albus, 214
  T. v. aurea, 214
  T. v. 'Silver Posie', 37, 41, 81
ties, raised beds, 92, 93, 249
tiles, raised flower bed, 92
Tilia platyphyllos 'Rubra', 120
tobacco plants, 64, 82, 85
tomatoes, 89, 207, 219, 223, 239
  baskets of tomatoes, 196–9
topiary, herb, 190–3
Trachelospermum jasminoides, 22
trees: circular pipe with flowering tree, 60–3
  in containers, 255
  planting, 251
  rose growing through, 182–5
  staking, 256
trellis, 108–11, 259
  rustic trellis, 112–15
  scented arbor, 124–7
  trellis-enclosed herb garden, 116–19
  trellis fence panel, 247
  trough with trellis screen, 22–5
  vertical planting, 120–3
  wood and trellis camouflage box, 10–13
  wooden obelisk, 128–31
Tropaeolum 'Alaska', 151
  T. majus, 219
troughs: brickwork trough, 82–5
  lead-faced trough, 52–5
  shell-faced trough, 48–51
  terra cotta with a patina, 68–71
  trough with trellis screen, 22–5
  vertical planting, 120–3
turnips, 89

V
vegetables: baskets of tomatoes, 196–9
  Asian vegetables, 228–31
  chile peppers in pots, 200–3
  edible border, 216–19
  patio container garden, 204–7
  potager, 236–9
  raised brick beds, 86–9

salad bed, 220–3
Verbascum bombyciferum, 101
Verbena, 123
  V. tenera, 120
  V. tenuisecta f. *alba*, 120
Veronica 'Shirley Blue', 101
Versailles cases, 14–17, 254, 255
vertical planting, 120–3
Viburnum, 186
Vinca minor, 22
  V. m. 'Alba Variegata', 51
  V. m. 'Azurea Flore Plena', 22
Viola cornuta, 101
  V. 'Jeannie Bellew', 168
  V. odorata, 186, 219
  V. tricolor, 151, 215
  V. x *wittrockiana*, 193
violets, Persian, 52

W
walls: brick walls, 248–9
  cold frames, 228–31
  raised beds, 86–93, 249
  retaining walls, 98–101
  sweet pea "wall," 177
  wall cascade, 102–5
washtub, painted galvanized, 64–7
water features, wall cascade, 102–5
watering: borders, 256–7
  chile peppers, 203
  containers, 255
  hanging baskets, 199
  herbs, 261
  salad crops, 222
  strawberry pots, 206, 207
wattle panels, 140–3
weeds, 250, 257
whitefly, 255
willowherb, white, 235
windbreaks, wattle panels, 143
window boxes: basic window box, 246
  herbal window box, 26–9
  lead-faced trough, 52–5
  raised scented window box, 34–7
  rustic window box, 56–9
winter protection: containers, 254
  exotic fruit trees, 211
winter savory, 119, 235
wires, supporting climbing plants, 180, 259
wirework basket, 156–9
Wisteria, 180, 259
  W. floribunda, 211
wood, 245
wood preservatives, 245
wood stains, 245
woodwork projects, 107
  balcony herb boxes, 38–41
  basic window box, 246

chamomile seat, 30–3
checkerboard parterre, 144–7
cold frames, 230–1
culinary herb half-barrels, 212–15
entrance containers, 18–21
herb staging, 148–51
herbal window box, 26–9
lead-faced trough, 52–5
miniature hurdles, 132–5
mitered corners, 247
picket fences, 136–9
primula theater, 152–5
raised scented window box, 34–7
rustic trellis, 112–15
rustic window box, 56–9
scented arbor, 124–7
tools, 244
trellis, 108–11
trellis-enclosed herb garden, 116–19
trellis fence panel, 247
Versailles case, 14–17
vertical planting, 120–3
wattle panels, 140–3
wood and trellis camouflage box, 10–13
wooden obelisk, 128–31
wormwood, 41

Y
yarrow, 235

Z
zucchini, 89, 207, 219

acknowledgments

In addition to the owners and establishments mentioned on page 265, the authors
would like to thank Jill Duchess of Hamilton for lending urns; Peter Goodwins
and Jack Bell for construction and bricklaying; and, for lending plants, Brian and
Rosemary Clifton-Sprig, John Powles at the Romantic Garden Nursery,
Swannington, Norfolk, and Jane Seabrook and The Chelsea Gardener.

Jane Seabrook also designed two projects: vertical planting on page 120 and the
wirework basket on page 156. The brick-edged herb garden (page 78) was designed
by Anthony O'Grady, head gardener at Penshurst Place, Kent. The herb-lined
pathway (page 94) was designed by Lucy Huntington. All other projects were
designed by the authors.

The six titles on which this book is based were edited by
Lynn Bryan, Caroline Davison, Toria Leitch, Sarah Polden,
and Marek Walisiewicz. Graphic design was by Liz Brown,
Ingunn Jensen, Mark Latter, and Paul Reid. Caroline Davison
and Larraine Shamwana helped with photoshoots.